A BLINK IN THE EYE

OF THE

GREAT BLUE HERON

An Educator's Journey of Discovery

Advance Praise

"In his writing, Pat gives us 'a rich experience and understanding of how the trials and tribulations of life experiences can be the blessings of our learnings.' Blessings, which include, 'loving, compassion, and joy.'"

Dr. Ron and Mary Hulnick, authors of *Remembering the Light Within* and *Loyalty to Your Soul*

"Pat Peake is a truly spellbinding storyteller. Every time I hear a story, whether autobiographical or fiction, I forget everything else and I am transported into a place where only the heart is seen and heart. I weep, I laugh, and most of all I am profoundly touched and transformed by his insights, as well as his deep understanding and love of people, both young and old."

Kamala Nellen, author of *Coaching for Champions*

"Patric Peake writes with raw sincerity; occurrences painted with emotion that tug at heartstrings, urging the reader to enter his world. He is a storyteller in the original sense, visiting the deeper aspects of humanity though authentic stories from his extraordinary life."

Mandy Jackson-Beverly, author of *A Secret Muse*, and *The Legend of Astridr: birth*

"Patric Peake's stories have the unique gift of unexpectedly worming their way into your heart, leaving you with the glow of goodness in action, and a yearning to follow the example. In praise of a good story (or storyteller), this is hard to excel."

William G. Short, Esq. Law Offices of William G. Short, President of Ojai Valley Morning Toastmasters

A BLINK IN THE EYE

OF THE

GREAT BLUE HERON

An Educator's Journey of Discovery

By

Patric Peake

For Jeff, Robert, and Lisa

PROLOGUE

At twelve years old, I decided that riding my bike to church on Sunday to find God just wasn't for me.

It wasn't working.

One Sunday, I lashed my fishing pole onto my bike and headed for Duck Creek instead…in a heavy rain. I ploughed through thick brush to the large willow tree that guarded the best spot in the creek for both the fishing and swimming. I'd caught a lot of crawdads there and swam in my underwear.

As I crept up to the creek, now swelled with rain, I felt his eye. Just to the other side of the willow trunk, as still as the tree itself, the Great Blue Heron stared at me. The rain had become a fine mist. I stared back. He was huge, magnificent, noble. The blues and grays of his feathers set off streaks of white and orange on his long, slender head and beak. My heart pounded in his presence. Time held its breath. I was transfixed. Then, just once, he blinked and turned his head slightly.

At that moment I felt it. The bigness. The peace beyond words. All that stuff that poets strain to capture. I found what I had been looking for those other Sundays.

In a slow, heavy beat, the Great Blue Heron waved farewell with a six-foot wingspan and left me in awe. My twelve-year-old mind couldn't figure out where the moisture on my cheeks came from. The rain had quit.

It was much later in life that I found the words that best described this experience:

> *God enters by a private door into*
> *every individual.*
> *-Ralph Waldo Emerson*

I would see the Great Blue Heron again and again in my life. It seemed that whenever I needed a reminder, he would fly across the horizon, or show up in my pasture, or even join me on a dock where I was fishing.

Everything I write and speak about comes

to me in much the same way as that bird did; as a gift. Each story represents a special blink in my life, a moment when I became just a little bit more aware of who we *really* are.

Not to spoil the ending…the answer is good news.

1

IN THE BEGINNING

And not in utter nakedness,
But trailing clouds of glory do we come
From God, who is our home:
Heaven lies about us in our infancy!

-William Wordsworth

"Who do you want us to save, your wife or the child?"

That's what the doctor asked a twenty-year-old man, very tired from long work days, who pondered this question for just ten seconds, running his fingers through his thick, dark hair. That was all the time he needed.

In the delivery room, the doctor announced the man's answer and they prepared to operate on this seventeen-year-old blonde with a face of a movie star. However, the child inside the man's wife had his own answer. No cutting. The delivery team was astonished as a foot came out, and then another. The child came out backwards, kicking. His answer was, "Save both of us."

And thus, I was born.

I am honored to share this book, my journey into the discovery of who we really are, with you. In a series of short, true-life stories, generally chronological, this book takes us through some significant signposts in my youth and lots of stories about my work with children and adults as an educator, especially stories of kids with tough lives and how they transcended their situations. It is a journey of the educator learning from the student.

It also takes us through the tough times and the sweet times as a devoted husband and loving father. It is a journey into a place inside of each of us that is much larger, much more magnificent than we could have ever imagined. Please join me. As an avid fisherman, I will do my best to catch your heart.

2

PLAYGROUND

*Whatever games are played with us, we must play
no games with ourselves.*

-Ralph Waldo Emerson

In my white T-shirt with the blue, stenciled
letters "PLAYGROUND DIRECTOR" on the
back, I skidded down the wet, grassy hill to Glen
Haven Playground. Some three acres of park was
created from land leveled over an old city dump
on the edge of the west side ghetto in Davenport,
Iowa. That was before the word "ghetto" really
existed; in the summer of 1962. The Glen Haven
residential area really fit the modern concept of a
ghetto; old run-down homes, children playing in
the streets in bare feet, and a crime rate that

warned folks to stay in their homes at night.

I was the first white male playground director they had ever seen, just eighteen years old. And I had a tough act to follow. Last summer's director was Gayle Hopkins, the only athlete from our town to make it to the Olympics.

Rita Peyton, my African-American colleague, was my one link with any sense of safety. I ran six-foot-four and about 160 pounds in those days. Rita probably weighed the same as me, but she was a good foot and a half shorter and ten years older. We looked about as compatible as a suntanned beanpole and an overripe eggplant.

By eleven that morning, I had deluded myself into thinking that playing checkers with a girl named Rakisha meant all was well. She was a slim preteen with a dark, thin face and huge eyes that made me smile. To add to this, she sang Motown tunes the entire time she played checkers, with a voice that belonged on the Apollo stage. Jimbo, our youngest kid at six, wrapped his arms around my neck establishing for the summer that my back was his personal recreational vehicle. That's when Henry and the boys came to the playground to remind me that life isn't just a game of checkers.

I was just eighteen and these nine boys were a year behind me in school. They chatted loudly, threatening each other with physical abuse, apparently unaware that I existed. However, occasionally they sniffed the air as if the wind was blowing the wrong way from the new city dump. I felt a rock growing in my gut. A couple of them did "show-and-tell" with their new pocket knives and pretended to demonstrate their artistic talent on a nearby picnic table.

Bored with this, they eventually cruised by me into the shelter to grab a basketball. I tensed like a sheriff in a saloon full of gunfighters and continued to play checkers. Rita wasn't going to be any help as she was with some little ones on the other side of the playground.

Without a word to me, they began a full-court game.

"Wasn't they supposed to check out that ball?" Rakisha stopped singing.

To be honest, I had no clue what to do. Their four-on-four street ball game on our new concrete court looked more like ice hockey with fake smiles. The ninth guy watched from the sidelines providing bathroom humor commentary with sound effects.

Boom! In yo face, sucker!

Meanwhile, I felt a sharp pinch on my arm. Rakisha pulled on the blond hairs of my very darkly tanned skin. Her eyes got big. "Pat!"

"Yes?"

"You a white boy!"

"Oh my gosh! Really?" I teased. My smile left as I glanced over my shoulder and took a deep breath. I figured the pinch was my wake-up call. Time to make my move. I shrugged Jimbo off my shoulders.

I walked over to the edge of the court and asked, "Mind if I play?"

Henry stopped the game by grabbing the ball in one hand and slapping it with the other. "Sure, if you think you can keep up, white boy." He was a big, stocky boy with an old sweatshirt cut off at the sleeves to show off his muscular biceps.

What I was sure of was that a white, second-string high school basketball player did not command the same respect as an Olympic athlete. They put me on the losing team, and then gave me Henry to guard. Henry was a middle lineman for the football team, not a basketball player. Nevertheless, he tried to give me a lesson in how to establish your rebounding territory called, "If you come in here, you die."

Still, I was hitting my shot and made a few good passes. The game was close. and it was time for Henry to make it clear to everyone who was going to win the game. I had good position for a rebound. He climbed my back like a step ladder and tapped in the ball while his knee dug into my spine. My insides burned with rage, which I knew I couldn't show. In this game, flagrant fouls were just part of the game, and I had to take it.

My turn.

At our end of the court, I posted in close to the basket and got the ball with Henry breathing down my neck. With my furious head fake, Henry leaped up in the air like he was getting ready to swat a fly. As he came down, I went up, my pencil-sharp elbow jabbing into Henry's gut. I made the layup as Henry made a huffing noise dropping to his knees on the concrete.

A five-second pause came. Henry's teammates awaited his retaliation. I kept playing like it was just all part of the game and, thank God, so did Henry. He picked himself up and played on. They won that game. That was okay. I had made my move.

After the game, Henry asked me if they could keep the ball over lunch. Rita blasted me for saying yes and told me I was a fool if I ever thought I was going to see that ball again.

When Rita and I got to our cars, Henry yelled at me, "Here, Pat, we decided not to play." And he tossed me the ball. The game was over. They didn't need to play with me anymore, not in that way.

3

GOLD

*For anything worth having one must pay
the price;
And the price is always work, patience,
love, self-sacrifice
— no paper currency, no promises to pay,
but the gold of real service.*

-John Burroughs

If you ask my wife about me, one thing she
may say is, "This man can step on a cow pie and
find the gold in it."

It wasn't always that way. At twenty years old,
I felt I pretty much knew all there was to know
and could handle anything that came my way.

Until I met Alan.

As the lead counselor for a cabin of eight young boys with Down syndrome, I greeted parents as they brought their boys for their first ever week of camp in the woods east of Waterloo, Iowa. I should have known by the guilty look on his parents' faces that Alan was not "camp ready," as per our guidelines. Never mind that he clung to his mom's leg like a pale-faced baby orangutan with red hair to match. Never mind that after we pried him off of her, he screamed "Mom! Mom! Mom!" for at least ten minutes after his parents had driven away. Never mind that he plopped onto his cot in the cabin like a sack of potatoes and refused to move. I was twenty, and knew everything.

Four other special needs cabins housed eight kids, each with a lead counselor and teen assistant. I had told Alan's parents, "Don't worry. We'll take good care of him." When they were gone, Freddy, my assistant, said, "What do you mean 'we?'" I realized at that moment, that Alan was all mine. But that was okay. I was twenty…

On the first day, you did not have to be an expert tracker to tell when my group traveled the trail. One distinct set of footprints walked backwards with a set of parallel furrows between them. That would be me, dragging Alan to his next activity. By the end of that day, "Mom! Mom! Mom!" became "Pat! Pat! Pat!" I was totally exhausted at tuck-in time, and Alan let me know that I would be sleeping in the cot next to his, or not at all.

Next morning, an hour before any human being should be required to be awake, I sat straight up in bed, with a pungent odor assaulting my nose. Yes, Alan, had definitely not been camp ready.

Thousands of people have changed the soiled sheets of thousands of other people so if they could, I could, I thought. But I wondered if theirs smelled as bad. I ate no breakfast.

The second day was better. Alan began to show signs that he could actually walk on his own and even occasionally shared *his* counselor Pat with the others. That night, we made sure everybody took care of business before bed.

Next morning, I awoke to Alan singing with the birds, and sitting in his latest deposit. He thought I was playing with him and giggled as I yanked the sheets from under him using them to wipe him. Freddy just looked at me like I was crazy and turned away to take care of the other campers.

At breakfast, watching Alan slurp his oatmeal, something snapped. I imagined snatching him by the arm and dragging him to the office to call his parents to come get him. Instead, I abruptly left the table and went out to the tether ball pole. I thought of Alan as I punched the yellow leather ball. I punched and punched and punched. Suddenly, under the fury that flew into those punches, I felt something else. Something like tears. Tears for Alan. Tears for the little guy inside me who did NOT know everything. I took a deep breath and returned to Alan and the boys.

The funny part is, that as something shifted inside me, it seemed like Alan changed. The next two mornings, clean sheets blessed us. Also, Alan's worm won one of the worm races I devised, and he shared his prize, a box of milk chocolate-covered caramels, with his tent mates.

On the last day of camp, Alan marched up to the stage and performed in our little skit for the camp program for parents. He spotted his mom. He did not hop off the stage to grab her leg. He just waved and said, "Hi Mom."

I am fairly certain that Alan's parents did not completely understand my response to their tear-filled thank you.

"No," I said, "I thank you."

I thank you, Alan, for the gift you gave me, for what you taught me, for your gold. Also, congratulations on your choice of worm.

4

FIRST CLASSROOM

Tenderness and kindness are not signs of
weakness and despair,
but manifestations of strength and resolution.

-Kahlil Gibran

Some boys stood on the chairs of their classroom desks making chicken noises. The shrill giggle of preteen girls assaulted my ears. A paper ball flew across the room. Chaos greeted me in my first paid teaching position, a seventh-grade homeroom class in El Paso, Texas. The previous teacher had resigned suddenly. I was beginning to suspect why.

My appearance seemed to have no impact on their behavior. I had on a black suit and tie, I was six-foot-four with a muscular frame, clean shaven, with short hair. One of my previous jobs was drill instructor for the United States Army. Couldn't they see this?

Then I spotted her. Lydia's large, brown eyes were the only thing steady in the room. She stared at me in silence.

Since the final bell hadn't rung yet, I pretended not to notice the continuing chaos, inventorying the stuff on my desk but glancing up to spot which students would need the most attention. I thumbed through the roll book putting names to faces.

I got up and printed "MR. PEAKE" in giant letters on the blackboard. There was no change in the noise level, but at least they were more or less in their seats. I leaned back in my chair, picking up a familiar novel for comfort, hoping they couldn't see my hands shaking. I looked up. The noise level had dropped only a decibel.

Lydia's silent eyes continued to study me. A friend sitting next to her chattered Spanish in her ear continually. But Lydia remained silent. She was tall, Latina, with sandy brown hair, fair skin and a gentle, serious face. She sat straight up in her chair and continued her unblinking gaze.

The bell to start class rang and I stood, noticing as I rose, that my knuckles had whitened on the arms of my chair.

They're all waiting for me to do something.

A strange voice inside cautioned me not to start barking orders.

Talk to that girl who is staring at you instead.

I walked over and sat in the empty chair next to the girl and her friend.

"Hi."

"She looked directly into my eyes and asked, "Are you a flower child?" It was 1965.

"A what?" I adjusted my tie.

She didn't repeat herself, so I asked, "What do you think makes a person a flower child?"

"Well," she said, "I think flower children believe in love and peace."

"Is that all?" I asked.

"Yep."

"Then I guess I'm a flower child. Are you?"

"No, I'm just Lydia." Her eyes remained serious.

"Well, Lydia, can you tell me what's going on here?"

She looked out at the rest of the class for the first time since I had entered the room. "They've been like this since they threw Mr. Bernardo out the window. He was crazy."

"Crazy? What does a teacher have to do to be called 'crazy' around here?" As I said that, I watched a boy jump from his chair flapping his elbows like they were wings. In a moment, he quieted and glided over to perch in a nearby desk.

Gradually, one-by-one, all twenty-seven students became silent and began migrating to our side of the room as Lydia and I talked. Some had to stand between desks to get a good spot. They each took a stab at answering my question. Mr. Bernardo kicked wastebaskets and threw books across the room. He gave the class long periods of "free time" which usually ended in his violent explosion of anger. He left four kids out in the hall once after paddling each one and forgot they were there until the end of the day. *I wondered where he kept the paddle.*

The students squabbled over who got to tell the

big story. Lydia took charge. She looked at my name on the blackboard. "So, Mr. Peake, one day Mr. Bernardo got really mad because Enrique tripped and knocked over his own desk. He fell hard and his stuff went everywhere. The boys all laughed. Some of the girls, too. Teacher went to *that* window." She pointed to the window by my desk. "He opened it, put his feet outside, and sat there on the windowsill shouting bad words at us."

"Yeah, Bernardo said, 'I don't have to take this shit!'" The red-headed boy laughed at himself along with several other boys in the class.

Lydia frowned at them. "That's when Enrique, Jose and Freddy charged the window and pushed him out. Mr. Bernardo landed on his behind. It must have hurt even though we're on the first floor. He used the 'F' word and walked away. We never saw him again."

When I checked this story later with staff, I found out Mr. Bernardo went directly to the faculty bathroom to clean up, took a piece of toilet paper and wrote, "I quit." He banged open the door to the principal's office, slapped the tissue on her desk, and disappeared.

Listening to Lydia and the others, a plan emerged. I said to them, "If I tell you a short story about something I saw once in the Army—"

"You were in the Army?" asked a Latino boy with highly polished black shoes.

"Yes, but I didn't actually fight in the war. I was a drill sergeant. The story I have is about a guy who did go to the war."

"Cool," said one of the other boys. "Tell it."

"If I do…" I looked at all of them. "Each of you has to write me a story about a topic of my choosing. Okay?"

Most of them nodded like bobbleheads in the rear window of a car.

"Well, this guy was the least friendly person I had ever met. He was a corporal, and I was his boss, a sergeant. He wouldn't even say 'hello' in the morning. He just sat there at the desk next to mine, waiting to go home. I found out from my boss that he had been a machine gunner on a helicopter in Vietnam."

"That's a cool job," a boy said. "My uncle—"

I put a hand up. "My story."

"Oh, sorry," he said.

"The guy would get mad over the littlest thing. Once I asked him to retype a report. I made some corrections and handed it back to him. Well, he said almost the same thing Mr. Bernardo did when he was in the window. He wadded up the report and tossed it at the wastebasket. He missed."

"What did you do?" Lydia's friend asked.

"Did you punish him?" asked the Latino boy with the shiny shoes.

"No." I glanced at Lydia. "I went over to the wastebasket, picked up the wad of paper beside it, smoothed it out, and retyped the report myself."

"Aww, man!" one of the boys said.

"I know why you did that," Lydia said.

"You probably do, Lydia," I said. "A few days later, he did something scary. I'm going to show you what happened. Watch."

I got up, walked over to my desk and took a ballpoint pen out of the cup of writing tools. I returned to the student desk beside Lydia. I knew I had their attention. They remained silent. I started tapping the back of the pen on my desk clicking and un-clicking it on the hard surface.

"My desk was next to his. I was thinking about something. I did this." I continued tapping hard and fast. Suddenly, the corporal screamed 'Incoming!' and dived under his desk. He stayed there. I told him I was sorry and got on my knees. He was under there shaking like a scared rabbit. His eyes were big and shifted back and forth really fast. 'It's okay,' I said to him. 'It's just my pen. I won't ever do that again.' It took me five minutes to talk him out of there."

I looked at my captured audience.

"From then on, I treated the corporal with an even deeper respect for what he'd been through. That's my story."

Comments were all short. "Whoa. Poor guy. Cool. Sad."

"So, your turn. Ready to write me a story?" I asked.

Bobblehead nods.

"Write me one page on what could have happened that was so bad, so sad, so hard, that it would cause someone to act crazy."

A couple of kids couldn't write, but really had a

story. They dictated theirs to Lydia, who wrote them down for them. Girls talked about cruel parents. Boys talked about tragic battles. By the end of class, they had all finished and were ready for their follow-up homework assignment:

Write a letter of apology to Mr. Bernardo. Most of them did. A few brought notes from their parents explaining to me why they would not.

After school that day, I heard a knock on my door. I looked up from reading the stories that they had written. "Come in."

In marched the boy with the shiny shoes. A the front edge of my desk he stood at attention. "I am here for my punishment, Sir." He looked high above my head.

"Punishment?"

"My swats, Sir. For talking in class." He continued to stare above me.

I turned and looked up. There it was.

"Soldier," I said, "Not on my watch. You're dismissed."

"Yes, Sir," he said. He blinked once, turned, and marched out.

It wasn't the size of the paddle that got to me.

It wasn't even the students names printed on it in permanent marker. It was the large holes bored into the paddle to create more pain.

I looked down at the story I was reading. It was Lydia's. At the bottom of the page was a P.S.

I knew you were a flower child.

5

WHAT A DEAD GUY I NEVER KNEW TAUGHT ME

Those we love never truly leave us, Harry.
There are things that death cannot touch.

- J. K. Rowling

Many years ago, my now ex-wife asked me to leave her and our son in El Paso, Texas, and never come back. I took the van with my few possessions, and drove north. Nothing made sense to me about anything in that time of sadness and loss. It felt like a death.

I chose two renowned therapists to work with; Dr. Nature and Dr. Fish. I drove through the lovely little town of Las Vegas, New Mexico and up into the Santa Fe National Forest. For a month, I camped out in my van, ate bread, beans and fish and drank coffee percolated on a little camp stove. I told my troubles to the squirrels and the fish. My problems were cleansed in the clear New Mexico streams.

When it was time to return to the world, I drove back down to the little town, went to a phone booth, opened to the yellow pages, and started making phone calls. I got as far as "Ambulance Driver."

Samuels Mortuary and Ambulance Service hired me. Besides driving an ambulance and cleaning the mortuary, I assisted in all aspects of the mortuary business. My pay was lodging in a two-room apartment above the mortuary, and seventy-five dollars every two weeks. I thrived on cornbread, beans and rice.

I did not thrive as well working with the bodies, preparing them for funerals or cremations. I let myself become too personally involved with the clients. The truth is I felt love for each departed soul. What had their lives been about? Who would cry at their funeral?

None touched me as deeply as my first

ambulance call, my first death call, and my first graveside funeral...all three, Juan Ramirez. This first call was supposed to be easy. Pick up Juan at the convalescent hospital and take him to the New Mexico State Mental Hospital just outside of town. I didn't stop to consider why he needed the transfer.

As I pulled the gurney up to Juan's bed, I was struck by how gaunt he looked. His cheeks sunken and arms like broomsticks, he looked barely alive.

I'd just worked a service at the mortuary so I still had on my black suit. When Juan saw this tall man in a black suit at his bedside he probably thought The Grim Reaper had arrived. He lunged and grabbed my arm with one hand, and my throat with the other, hurling curses at me in Spanish. For a man with little flesh left on his bones, he had the grip of a pit bull. I had to get assistance in prying his hands from me. For a man so near death, he seemed so desperate to live.

I delivered him to the hospital, with his arms strapped to the gurney. He looked so frightened and confused as they took him. He bent his arm at the restraints and held out a hand to me, and I took it and squeezed. Amidst frowns from the attendants, I departed. My first ambulance call was in the books.

Less than a week later, I received my first death call, Juan. When they let me in the state hospital through the double-locked doors, I naively wheeled my gurney to his room. His bed was made and vacant. The attendants rolled their eyes at each other as they guided me to the freezers. Juan's body hadn't been in there long. My boss, the mortician, was glad to see this because it meant he could get the embalming done right away. With the process completed, his body was placed into a simple pine coffin, and I was left to do the clean up.

I pushed back the lid and looked him over. By his rough hands and ruddy skin, I was pretty sure he'd been a rancher, maybe a real cowboy, a *vaquero*. In my own way, I spoke a little prayer to Juan. I told him I hoped his life had been a good one.

Juan was also my first graveside funeral. He

was buried in a cemetery with just a few headstones, mostly just slabs on the ground, down a small gravel road in a field behind the state hospital. The attendees of Juan's funeral were two maintenance men from the hospital, a priest, and me.

I didn't understand the words the priest spoke, but it felt sacred, honoring the passing of a human life. It struck my heart. I began to weep silently and continued to weep all the way back to the funeral home. Juan had let go of his grip on life. My weeping turned to deep sobbing when I realized that, like Juan, I'd let go of a life. In that time of letting go, we were both alone.

At that point, I found myself beginning to connect with people who were alive, reaching out with the same hand of kindness I extended to Juan, sharing my life with them.

That evening, as I was cleaning, I found Juan's belt in the supply room. It had a cool silver belt buckle with a cowboy riding a bucking bronco on it. I decided that Juan would want me to have his belt, his legacy. I wore it proudly for many years.

Long after that funeral, I visited that graveyard

and looked for Juan's slab. I wanted to thank him, but I never found it. He's still in my heart. Juan taught me the sanctity of all our precious lives and the importance of a caring connection with each person I meet. Like the song by Jewel says, *"In the end, only kindness matters."*

Adios, Juan. Thanks for our brief time together. Thanks for the big lesson you taught me. And, of course, thanks for the cool belt.

6

THE FIRST TIME EVER

The very first moment I beheld him, my heart was irrevocably gone.

-Jane Austen

Still in my black suit from ushering a recent funeral, I heard a knock at the door of my apartment above the mortuary. I opened it to three teen girls looking up at me with skeptical faces. They were student editors, with whom I would be working in my new job as high school journalism teacher. The school principal had called to see if they could come over and ask a few questions.

"Nice to meet you."

The brunette flushed, her dark brown eyes emanated an electric energy. *Was she angry?* The two blondes just crossed their arms in front of them. They were here to check out my qualifications. I'd been given the task of replacing the long-time, beloved journalism teacher and finding someone to publish the school newspaper more cheaply due to budget cuts.

Chatting with the girls, I felt like a used car salesman trying to invent reasons for buying, in this case, me! They didn't smile on their way out. The dark-haired girl cast a last cynical glance over her shoulder at me. Her name was Margaret.

I knew that my teaching methods wouldn't be as by-the-book as the previous teacher. I had been editor of my college paper and wrote for a couple of local papers. As the students and I began working together, I was able to develop a modicum of, if not respect, at least tolerance.

But there was a problem when it came time to get the first edition of the school newspaper published. The print shop I found, thirty miles away, was run by some monks who didn't drive. The deadline for copy was that day, and we had fifteen stories with no headlines written. In my panic, I asked the co-editor Ellen to ride with me in my van and write headlines on the way to the printer. The school principal caught wind of my plan and called me in. I still remember his words.

"Mr. Peake, you will not be driving anywhere with one female student in your van. You call Margaret out of class and have two girls riding with you."

To my relief, the ladies actually enjoyed this unusual journey into the Pecos Mountains, writing great headlines, and meeting a monk in a long brown robe who took our copy as if it were a sacred manuscript.

The Monk's offset machine and printing of the paper was a bit off. The newspaper looked more like one of those ransom notes pasted together from the type in various periodicals. Thankfully, after the local printer discovered there was competition, he brought down his prices.

Margaret actually became fond of my somewhat out-of-the-box educational strategies. I even made her laugh once in a while. She won a couple of journalism awards that year. We published eight quality editions of the newspaper and a yearbook.

Just after graduation that year, divorce papers were served to me. A month later, my wife and son moved away with her new husband. I lived in a little house beside the mortuary where I used to work.

Two years later, toward the end of summer, Margaret appeared at the screen door. As she walked through, my heart pounded. David, a visitor and also a former student, saw and felt the intensity of the look between us and invented a reason to leave quickly. Her steady, brown eyes gazed directly at me. Her matching hair hung straight down, spilling below her shoulders. She wore jeans and a flannel shirt, and I was struck by her simple, genuine beauty. I felt both terrified and embarrassed by my own feelings

Teachers are not supposed to have these feelings for their students.

We talked, and talked, and talked about writing and psychology and the meaning of life. We took a walk to a local park and talked some more. When we were silent, the feelings in me became overwhelming. I would say something, and we'd talk more.

Returning to my living room, she pulled out her car keys and said she had to head home.

"Well, gosh, Margaret, I'm so glad you visited. Thanks for the great talk. I hope you'll visit again."

After my awkward invitation, she said something that changed my life forever.

She stopped in my doorway, turned back, her sparkling brown eyes smiling at me, and said, "I have a phone."

Forty-five years later, as I write this, I will probably be getting a call or text from her, my wife, Margaret, seeing if I'm still at the coffee shop writing. Her call will make me smile. I remember what she told me several years into our marriage about that first time she met me. She said she'd had a disturbing thought when she saw me in my black suit.

What a strange-looking man. I wonder if I will marry him someday.

I did call Margaret that next morning and it led to an all-day date. That evening we heard a song by Roberta Flack on the jukebox at a local pizza place. It became our song.

"The first time ever I saw your face, I thought the sun rose in your eyes..."

I still do.

7

TO JOSE

Education is the ability to listen to
almost anything
without losing your temper or your
self-confidence.

-Robert Frost

Have you ever had someone come up to you and say, "You might not remember me, but you did something or said something that changed my life forever?"

Jose changed mine. It happened in a high school math classroom in New Mexico in the spring of 1968. Besides journalism, I also taught math.

Jose rose from his desk pulling a small baseball

bat from the sleeve of his oversized sweatshirt. He literally climbed over three rows of desks filled with students, and swung that bat at the head of Mario.

Now Jose weighed maybe a hundred pounds dripping wet, so when I caught his wrist mid-strike, I was able to wrap my other arm around his waist and carry him and the bat out of the classroom. I motioned to a teacher on his prep period to take my class and stood Jose against the hall lockers.

He slumped to the floor and sat, releasing his weapon which rolled across the gray tile to the other side of the hall. I sat beside him. Head down, he stared at his shoes. His sunken, large brown eyes gleamed in the hall light reflecting off the linoleum floor.

"He must have said something pretty bad," I said.

"He called my father a *cabron*."

"I hear you," I said, and actually, I heard much more. His father had been campus security at the local university and had recently passed away.

As I began exploring strategies to turn this

event into something constructive, Mr. Samson, the school vice principal, trumped my efforts.

"What in hell are you doing out here with him, Peake?"

What followed was the verbal beating of Jose followed by his expulsion from school. No options. I tried to explain the circumstance but was met with a glare, "We'll talk in my office ... later." That meeting was like me trying to tell a penguin there's another color besides black and white. It's called grey.

Now you may say that Mr. Samson did the right thing, despite how he may have done it. The safety of the students is important, and I absolutely would agree...except for the no options part. Jose was still a human being, and we were still educators. That afternoon, I tendered my resignation effective at the end of the school year in one month. I thought I might never teach in another public school.

That summer, as I walked out of my very last university class session to complete my master's degree in school counseling, my instructor, Dr. Gonzalez ran up to me, knowing I had resigned

"Hey, Peake. How'd you like to run a school in Calexico, California where the kids are so bad, they don't care how you run it?"

A week later I stuck out my thumb on the highway and got a ride westward to Gallup, New Mexico from a Navajo Indian in the back of his truck. I tried my thumb for hours from Gallup with no luck; so, I took a Greyhound to Phoenix. From there, at two in the morning, I got a ride from Earl, who had just gotten out of county jail.

Earl had that weathered look about him, eyes narrowing as if the enemy lay behind the next rock, stubbly facial hair, strands of long, unwashed blondish hair streaming down his cheeks. I knew his story would not be pretty.

He told me that story as he drove, a tale of one train wreck after another, never his fault. Like the time his wife called the cops for him hitting her when *she* was the one who went out on him. Still, I listened carefully and with compassion. As he got deeper into the sadness of his story, he decided he needed a drink. He turned the wheel over to me so he could drink, and drink, and drink some more.

By the time we reached the Imperial Valley desert, it was dawn, and he needed to take a leak. It was 112 degrees. I stopped the car on the sandy shoulder. He found a large cactus behind which he could conduct his business. As he returned, he bent over and pulled something out of his boot.

The ten-inch blade of a hunting knife gleamed in the sun, pointed at me.

"You were gonna drive off without me!"

"Earl," I said. "No way. Remember me. Remember how you told me about..." and I recapped some of his story. It seemed to calm him down. Being heard can do that, fortunately. He hopped back in, and I drove.

I pulled off onto the side of the freeway near the first exit to El Centro, California, and turned the car over to him with a silent prayer for his well-being. I lugged my large briefcase about a mile in the heat to the Greyhound station. The dry heat evaporated my sweat so fast that all I was left with was the salt and the smell.

At the bus station, I went to the bathroom sink and washed off as much as I could. I went to a stall and changed into the clean shirt and suit coat

I had folded into my briefcase, and purchased a five-dollar bus ticket to the border town of Calexico, California a few miles away.

Thirty minutes later, I interviewed for the job of principal of Calexico Continuation High School, which we later that year named Aurora High School.

Twenty years later, I was running that school, which had grown from twenty-five kids with train-wreck stories like Earl's, to 200 kids who mostly discovered how to get back on the tracks.

I think I've learned to be a pretty good listener. I've heard what my teachers had to say. I've heard the kids and all their various stories. Along the way, I've been blessed with so many special connections.

So I want to say, thank you Jose. In that time sitting on the hallway floor with you, you taught me to look for the love often hiding under the anger. You changed my life forever.

8

HOPE

To love, and bear; to hope till Hope creates from its own wreck the thing it contemplates...

-Percy Bysshe Shelley

How do we find hope in dark times?

Magdalena was a sweet girl. Frankly, I wondered how she ended up at Aurora High School for high-risk teens. Her parents were supportive and even fixed a nice Mexican dinner for the entire staff at the beginning of the school year.

One day, after school, she came and sat in the chair next to my desk, folded her hands on her lap, and looked at me. Well, actually, she looked through me. I'd never seen such darkness as I saw in her eyes.

"You have something to tell me, Magdalena?"

"Yes." She looked down at her stomach.

After an uncomfortably long pause, I asked, "Would you like to tell me now?"

"My Papa. He is very sick from the heart. Very sick."

"I'm sorry to hear that, Magdalena."

The tears began to roll silently down her stony face and she said, "There's more."

"More?"

"Mr. Peake, I'm pregnant." Now the tears really flowed.

I remained silent not knowing what to make of it, or what she made of this news.

"If Papa finds out, it will kill him."

"I see," I said. "Who have you told about this?"

"Nobody."

"Your mom?"

"No."

She explained that the boy who did this was there for just one day and moved on. I felt lost. What could I say to this sweet young lady?

"I am so sorry." I tried to meet her eyes.

"Me, too." She looked down.

All I could think to do was to refer her to someone who might know better how to help her.

"Mrs. Gonzalez is our district psychologist and a very nice lady. Would you like to talk with her?"

"No."

"How about Father Bryant?"

She paused.

"He works a lot with teens."

"I will tell Father Bryant." She looked away.

"When?"

"Tonight at confession."

"Okay, Magdalena. I want you to know I am going to check with Father Bryant tomorrow. Okay?"

"Sure." Her eyes glossed over.

"Sure?"

"I will."

I didn't believe her. I alerted the school psychologist, and she said she would make an appointment with Magdalena for the following day.

My secretary greeted me the next morning.

"Mr. Peake did you hear…about Magdalena?" Even before she said her next words, the rock had already hit my chest. "She committed suicide."

In a school of fifty students and four teachers, that kind of news stops all attempts at formal education and brings up long conversations and conjectures about what had happened. Word was she overdosed on her dad's heart medication… after he died of a heart attack.

I was lost. I had not a clue about how to recover from the guilt I felt. I should have called her parents. I should have called 911. I should have known what to do or what to say.

That same night I read in the paper that Dr. Elisabeth Kubler-Ross was giving a workshop based on her book about the stages of grief, *On Death and Dying*, at our local junior college. That weekend, my entire staff and I attended. She told us story after story of how people have evolved through the stages: Denial, Bargaining, Anger, Sadness, Acceptance, and finally, the one that was hardest to accept, Hope. There was such wisdom in Dr. Ross's eyes and in her words, such compassion for the human condition. "If we knew better, we would do better."

At the end of the workshop I gave this tiny, but powerful lady a warm hug.

Now, I can't say that because of her workshop I found hope in the story of Magdalena, but I did continue my quest to find answers. I studied grief counseling. I started a peer counseling class in my school, training a group of teens in basic listening skills, by having them listen to each other's real problems. We studied peer mediation and went over the stages of grief.

Word spread about our work and pretty soon, we were getting phone calls asking my peer counselors and me to show up at various schools because of one crisis or another.

I remember one call in particular. A high school senior was driving herself and her freshman brother to school in the family pick up. The truck overturned. She received minor scrapes, but her brother died. The district superintendent called me in to speak at an assembly and have my peer counselors there to support those closest to the popular young man.

I spoke in the assembly about the various ways

people grieve and about the importance of accepting their classmates in whatever way each person dealt with this loss. I told them that it's a time for coming together, not judging. We took the group who identified themselves as close to the boy to the far end of the bleachers and sent everyone else back to class. Some fifty students gathered together, my ten peer counselors dispersed among them, arms around shoulders of those with tears in their eyes.

One by one, they took turns talking about their feelings, their memories, their confusion. I noticed one girl standing against the wall just off to my right. She stared straight ahead, arms folded, frozen, like a statue. I noticed her eyes and saw that same dark look I'd seen on Magdalena's face. It was clear that she was not ready to speak to anyone. I asked the group who she was. They said she was the sister's best friend. She was right behind them driving and saw the whole thing.

I walked over to her and asked her if she would like to join the group.

She shook her head no.

"Are you okay?"

"Sure." She turned her head away, just like Magdalena did when she said she would contact her priest. I felt the pain of that memory in my chest.

"Well," I said. "If you could talk about it a little, it might help." I caught her glancing back at me as I started to walk away.

"I was there," she said.

I turned back and leaned on the wall beside her keeping a respectful distance. "And?"

"I was holding her. She was crying. I...I saw them put her brother in the bag. She asked me, 'Is my brother going to be all right?' And..."

She started breathing deep breaths.

"And?" I said.

"And I lied to her. I told her, her brother was okay." She broke into sobs and accepted my hand on her shoulder. Soon she joined her friends in the bleachers, arms wrapping around her from both sides.

I felt the pain in my chest ease up as I saw the color return to her face, the light back into her eyes. I must admit, I thought a bit about the sister of the dead boy. I wish I could somehow let her know that her truck turning over was an accident. Not her fault. That we can get through it. That maybe there really is hope.

Maybe I will someday…maybe when I stop blaming myself about Magdalena.

9

RIGOBERTO

*Do I not destroy my enemies when I make them
my friend?*

-Abraham Lincoln

I only know of two guys who got thrown out of
the game because of just a look. One was the
coach of an NBA basketball team. The other was
Rigoberto.

The coach's mouth stayed closed. It really did.
Twisted? Yes. Jaws bulging? Yes. Cheeks bright
red? Yes. But his mouth was closed.
Unfortunately, his eyes were extremely
expressive. They sent a hostile message to the
referee. It wasn't even about the call. It was
beyond that. The message in his eyes that got him

thrown out of the game said, *"I will kill you for that."*

The same message was in Rigoberto's eyes the day I dismissed him from school permanently. He verified this with me sixteen years later.

Rigoberto was the first student I ever kicked out of school. It was in my first year as principal of the continuation high school in Calexico. Ironically, in my very first talk with Rigoberto my first day on the job, I remember him telling me, "You probably just took this job so you could write a book about us." I was indignant that he could think such a thing.

So why did I kick him out? I really didn't know for sure. Can "sarcasm" be enough of a reason? How about cruising through remedial schoolwork and laughing at me as he did? Or his knowing kids were doing heroin in the bathroom and making jokes about it? Or how about being released from the juvenile criminal ward of a mental hospital, and acting like I was the one who was crazy? I didn't know. He was standing in the middle of the hallway watching me, a young, first-year principal listening to a teacher's complaint about him. His brown eyes gleamed at me with a huge smirk on his face. I lost it.

"You're nineteen years old and think this school is a big joke. You're *out*."

For Rigoberto, that wasn't enough of a reason to be *out*.

Sixteen years later, I heard Rigoberto's distinctive voice in the front office talking to the secretary. "Tell Peake I have something to discuss with him." My neck stiffened and my pulse quickened.

My secretary said, "Just a minute, I'll see if he's free."

My door banged open.

He hadn't changed much, I thought. The same deep, sunken, black eyes lurked under his dark eyebrows like a panther lurking under a bush. He had the same large presence, with a broad, flat face, muscular build, and a deep intellectual-sounding voice. And those eyes looked through you and around you but never at you.

"You know, Peake, I was going to kill you."

He surveyed everything in my office like he always did, his way of saying, *"You got a lot of valuable stuff here.*" Rigoberto taught me how to open a locked bathroom door when we thought a female student might have overdosed in there.

"Was?" I said. "What...what changed your mind?"

"Well, you know Freddy, a student you had last year?"

I nodded. I knew exactly who Freddy was and how much of a pain in the butt he'd been. The boy was even more arrogant than Rigoberto. But we managed to get him to crack a book once in a while, and one of our female teachers connected with him. I followed her advice when it came to Freddy.

"Well, I watched how you treated Freddy, and I decided that you're okay. I heard everybody talk about Mr. Peake. Mr. Peake this and Mr. Peake that, but I figured you were just a fake. But Freddy, well, he isn't easy...and you treated him the right way."

"Does Freddy know that you're his real dad?" It was an educated guess.

"No. I think he suspects, though."

Rigoberto went on to outline some of the ways

he had planned to kill me; the various weapons, locations, etc. I choose not to describe the gory details of his plans here. It's why I don't follow the news. He added that he got his high school diploma by test. "But you know Peake, that wasn't right what you did?"

"Yeah, I know. I never even gave you a chance to make it right."

"Exactly." He shared a rare grin. "I was playing with you, Peake. You know that."

"Now." I said.

"Right." He nodded, and left.

Less than a year later, I got a call from him late in the day after all staff had left.

"Hi, Peake. I'm dying."

I wasn't surprised by his news. Several of his classmates were dead. I had been to too many funerals. The term "high-risk teen" isn't a metaphor. At thirty-seven, drugs and alcohol had already killed Rigoberto's liver. The doctors gave him a month. He'd stopped working a week before, and had come home to die.

We talked a long time, in fact, so long that I got a "Where are you?" phone call from my wife on another line, a really appropriate question in that moment. During my talk with Rigoberto, we seemed to be outside of time and space, like that sacred moment when the Great Blue Heron blinked at me. We talked of old friends who'd died and friends who'd lived, as well. We talked of relatives. His son had gone to prison and found out about his real dad from the inmates. We talked like ancient warriors who had been through battle together. We pointed to our wounds. We proclaimed our victories. In the end, all that was important was that we were talking. The war was over between Rigoberto and me.

The guys from school surely talked about me at Rigoberto's funeral. They must have asked, "Where's Peake? He always comes to the funerals." That was one funeral I just couldn't make myself to go to. God Bless you, Rigoberto. Thank you. You were right about the book.

10

CINDERELLA

If Cinderella's slipper fit perfectly,
Why did it fall off?

-Anonymous

In the early days of Aurora High School, all students had to pass between my secretary, Aurora Pinto, and myself. We would often innocently tease as students came through to see if we could get a laugh out of them. Most got the joke.

If anyone had a reason *not* to get the joke, it was Carlos. His mom and dad both dead, he lived with his older brother in a one-room converted garage in the back by an alley.

Yet Carlos always got the joke...and had one to

give. "Hey, Mr. Peake, you know what? Eva sure likes her sugar in the morning. She poured the coffee into the sugar bowl and drank it. That's some sweet girl, huh?" He grinned from ear to ear and watched my face for a reaction. We all knew at my school that sugar addiction was a symptom of addiction to other substances.

Carlos was the only guy at our school who didn't do drugs. He was also the only guy in the school with a butch haircut. A short, stocky boy, his broad face displayed an enormous smile. He always wore slacks and a carefully ironed shirt, which he buttoned to the top. Unlike the other boys at our school, he was not hiding neck tattoos. Carlos was the only boy who graduated that year, my first year, from Aurora.

At the beginning of the next year, Carlos paid a visit with a special request. "Mr. Peake, I have this girl from Mexicali I want to marry. Will you help us get married?"

"Huh?"

"How do I do it?" he asked.

"Do what?

"Have you had your coffee yet this morning,

Peake?" He grinned.

"So you want to marry her here? In the U.S.?"

Carlos went to the coffee pot in the reception area and poured coffee. He returned and set it on my desk. He held out the sugar bowl. "Sugar?"

"Okay, okay, I get it. Not on drugs here. First, you go to the courthouse in El Centro and get a marriage license."

"Is there a bus to there from here?"

"Yes."

"When does it leave?" Carlos grinned.

"Whenever you tell me to." Knowing full well that *bus* meant my car, I couldn't say no to my first ever male graduate.

That afternoon I watched him put the cash in the teller window for an Imperial County marriage license. A few days later, at the border-crossing, Carlos, the bride and her mom piled into my Volkswagen bug to go to a wedding. He sat up front and I whispered to him. "How old is she?"

He grinned. "Fifteen."

I had nothing to say, but I'm sure Carlos saw the look of concern on my face.

As we squeezed out of my little car, Maria, the bride, whispered something to Carlos in Spanish.

"You know what, Mr. Peake, Maria thought you would be driving one of those black limos." He grinned with raised eyebrows.

We were told that their ceremony would happen during a recess from a traffic court session. The judge came out into a small, empty courtroom wearing a black robe.

The bride wore dark slacks and a nice, pale pink blouse. Shiny black hair, sparkling brown eyes, ruby red lips and high cheek bones, combined to create her classic Latina beauty. The groom wore slacks and a short sleeved blue shirt which he buttoned to the top button. Mom wore a mom's dress, the kind with little flowers. I wore my black suit, white shirt and tie, my chauffeur's uniform.

The wedding party of four stood roughly where a lawyer would stand. The judge stood before us. It was then that I noticed the bride's tummy. It moved.

The ceremony took about three minutes and included a thin, gold ring, brief vows, the signing of the marriage certificate, and a donation to the judge of $100, which is what someone told Carlos to give. The judge refused the gift with a warm smile. "You'll probably need that more than I do."

During the brief ceremony, Mom and I cried. The groom beamed with pride. The bride was a very sweet and pretty girl. However, she looked puzzled.

My final chauffeuring job was to return them to the border. The wedding party would cross to get her things and the bride would return with Carlos and move in. On the way to the border, I heard the new bride question her mom, who gave me an embarrassed grin through the rearview mirror. Carlos smiled, struggling not to laugh.

"You know what, Mr. Peake? You know what Maria asked her mom, Mr. Peake? She asked her 'When does the wedding start?'"

I checked out Maria in the mirror. As her mother explained it to her, our Cinderella smiled sheepishly. But she was content. She knew for certain that she had truly married her Prince Charming.

Ten years later, on a Sunday, I passed through Calexico with a bucket of catfish I'd caught in the canals. To my surprise, I spotted Carlos sitting on a lawn in front of a nice house with three beautiful, brown-eyed, black-haired little girls jumping all over him.

"Hey, Mr. Peake. How are you? This is Tina, and Luisa, and this little monster..." He tickled her as she pounced on him, "...is my oldest, Maria. Carlos beamed.

Out came Carlos' bride with that same content smile. She greeted me in broken English. I stayed long enough to clean the catfish in their backyard and give them twelve nice fillets. Carlos told me that he drove a school bus. Maria took care of the kids and went to night school. Grandma came out of the back room smiling. She nodded at me saying something to Carlos that made him laugh.

"She's says you're the man who was at the wedding that the bride missed."

Ah, I thought. *The bride may have missed her wedding, but the slipper fit perfectly.*

11

SECOND CHANCES

Second chances are not given to
make things right.
But are given to prove that we could be better
even after we fall.

-Charlie Chaplin

Does everyone deserve to have a second chance?

Continuation schools were specifically designed for second chances. We took high-risk teens who were challenged and challenging in the regular high school and gave them a second chance. How high risk was our school? Well, I sat in a courtroom once looking at the sawed-off shotgun that one of my students used to shoot and kill another of my students. The district attorney who was waving this weapon at me asked me the wrong question. He asked me if I believed there could be anything good about a boy who used this gun to shoot and kill another boy.

My answer was, "Yes. Of course."

I don't know what happened to the boy who held that gun. But I do know what happened to another boy who also knew about guns, Humberto.

All three of his male teachers called a meeting with me to complain about Humberto. "Peake, that boy has to go. He is completely obnoxious, totally defiant of male authority, and is destroying our classes."

"Right," I said. "So, if he asks for our newly created Second Chance Program, what would it take for him to return to your classrooms?"

It was almost a choral response. "A complete personality change!"

Humberto did go for that second chance.

"Yeah," he said, folding his arms in front of his chest, as he stood at my desk and looked out the window. He had a long, full face with lifeless, grayish, mannequin eyes and a chunky body. "Mom says I do your stupid program so I can get back into school or I find a new place to live."

"I'm moved by your enthusiasm." I handed him a sheet with the first topic of a Journal Writing Class, the class I used to get a clue about the kid. I told him to bring it in completed tomorrow and we'd talk about his service project.

The first topic for boys was to write about their father. How they were like their father and how they were different. The next day, he tossed this onto my desk and looked away:

Hey, Mr. P, I cant really say to much about my dad cuz when i five year old my mom bringt this man in our house She say to me watch this and the man he pull out a gun and shot my dad dead so i dont know nothin about him.

Humberto glanced down at me with a blank look.

I bit my lip and told him to come back tomorrow for his service project. As I read that journal, I thought of Mr. Lerner. He was a former teacher in juvenile hall, well-liked by his students, and was now living his last days in a convalescent hospital. Both of his legs were amputated as a result of diabetes. He had no family.

I made arrangements, and the next day I told Humberto that his service project was to visit Mr. Lerner for two hours each day, Monday through Friday. I told him his job was to be there for him in whatever way Mr. Lerner wanted.

He asked me, "How long?"

I said, "Until he dies. He's expected to live less than three months. And then, you must go to his funeral."

I watched Humberto calculate. "Okay."

Three days later, I heard Humberto yelling in the front office. He threw open my door.

"Peake, this is a bunch of f---ing s---! Gimme another project. I can't do this!"

"Good morning, Humberto, nice to see you, too. What's the problem?"

"F---ing Peake, I go in there and read the paper to him, and he don't even know who I am. He thinks I'm his son. He talks to his son, not me.

And he doesn't even *have* a son. "F--- ing Peake!"

I just looked at him and waited.

In a few seconds, his shoulders started shaking up and down. A high, faint whistling sound came out of his mouth. A gold chain rattled around his neck disappearing into the "v" of his shirt.

"New chain?"

He re-buttoned the top button. "Old. Real old."

I had a good idea where that came from but thought better of bringing it up then.

"Humberto, Mr. Lerner is not there to make you feel better. You're there for him. You have your service project. Go finish it. Or go home."

I checked with my friends on the staff at the convalescent hospital. Humberto not only visited Mr. Lerner on weekdays. He went on weekends also. They told me he had started helping out other patients as well. I didn't want Humberto to know I was checking up on him, but I had to make a short stop at Mr. Lerner's room during my regular Sunday visits to the facility.

Around Mr. Lerner's neck something gleamed.

"Where'd you get the gold chain, Mr. Lerner?"

He could barely speak, but raised a bent finger

at a small picture of Humberto on his bedside table. "My son." He closed his eyes and drifted into sleep.

A month later, the day after Mr. Lerner's funeral, which Humberto attended, he entered my office. To say he looked different would be an understatement. His softened eyes met mine. "Mr. Peake, do I get back in, Sir?"

"Just have one question for you. Where's your dad's gold chain?"

"It's with Mr. Lerner."

I announced to the teachers that Humberto was back. He had met their requirements for return.

The three male teachers just laughed and walked together to class, probably discussing my sanity. I made sure Humberto's schedule included each of them. By the end of that first day, each of Humberto's teachers came up to me individually and basically asked the same question. "How did you do it?"

"I didn't," I said. "Mr. Lerner did."

Does everyone deserve a second chance? Yes, everyone.

12

HEADLINES: 1981

Headlines, in a way, are what mislead you
because bad news is a headline,
and gradual improvement is not.

-Bill Gates

Who knows what the front page headlines were yesterday?

Not me. I don't read the newspaper. I don't watch the news. I *do* have a degree in journalism. So what's wrong with me? I began my journey away from the news in 1981 and have watched and read less and less news as I have grown older. Why 1981? Let me share three headlines I read that year:

Imperial Valley News Headline, Front Page, 1981:

"Anwar Sadat Assassinated"

What was *not* a front page headline, years earlier, was that Anwar Sadat won the Nobel Peace Prize and said, "Peace is much more precious than a piece of land..."

Imperial Valley News Headline, Front Page, 1981:

"Pope John Paul II Shot"

What was *not* a front page headline weeks later was that the Pope had a talk with his would-be assassin. He pardoned the man and referred to him as his brother.

Imperial Valley News Headline, Front Page, 1981:

"Aurora High School Burned to the Ground"

The night before I read that headline I had been reading some inspirational passages. I remember distinctly the message of one discourse which said that the things of this world will go away. Better to store up your treasures, put your heart into that which lasts, the love.

At two in the morning, I was jolted awake by the phone. As the principal of a continuation high school for at-risk teens, I was sort of used to these early morning calls. Once, a kid called me in the wee hours from prison.

"Hey, Peake, you were right about that when you told me nothing good happens after eleven at night. They busted me at eleven thirty."

Then there was the girl whose best friend had just attempted suicide.

And the kid who called me at three a.m. from a mental hospital.

"Shouldn't you whisper?" I asked.

He laughed. "Nobody sleeps here. Listen." He held the phone for me to hear what sounded like a busy shopping day at the mall.

But this call wasn't from one of my kids. It was from my boss, the superintendent. He said, "You better get down here, Peake. Your school's in flames."

By three in the morning, I was sitting on a picnic bench with my superintendent watching the tall orange flames consume my office, the outer office, the library, the restrooms and four of the six classrooms of Aurora High School. In a weird way, it was a beautiful sight. There was a tall palm tree that served for years as a measure of the height of the flames. It was charred a good thirty feet up its trunk. As I watched, I didn't dare tell my boss what was going on in my head. I had one thought, one clear and present thought.

I wonder what wonderful things are going to come out of this event.

Headlines in the *Imperial Valley News* did not see this event in quite the same way. They reported the suspected arson, which it was, and they played it up as a horrible malicious disaster.

Fresh from some inspirational classes and workshops with The University of Santa Monica and Insight Seminars, I saw the burning of my school as nothing less than a wonderful opportunity to turn a challenge into a blessing. I attempted to convey this to my staff. They looked at me like I belonged in that mental hospital.

Modular trailers were ordered to replace the classrooms. Meanwhile, we crammed all the seventy-five students into one of the remaining rooms for three hours a day for a week. I gave a personal growth workshop with the students and let the teachers spend the week inventorying the losses and regrouping. The only part of the rebuilding process that I could not quite embrace as an opportunity was the porta potties. They were gross.

The trailers came, and we were back in business. More students came as well. We worked hard with the students in those trailers while reconstruction began. In fact, we had an unusually good bunch of students, very motivated, and teachers to match.

During this time, one boy named Frank hung around my office, sometimes just to shoot the breeze. There was nothing special about Frank, except that he was a good guy who stayed clear of drugs and gangs. Frank didn't have a dad, and one day he asked me if I'd teach him to fish after school. Well, any excuse was a good excuse for fishing. I made a call.

"Honey, I'll be home late. This kid at my school wants to learn to fish. I think it will be good for him."

My wife replied, "Good for *him*?"

"Yes," and I took the boy fishing.

At the end of the year, I read two inches of news print written about the Aurora High School graduation, which was not on the front page. What was missing from the article was that in 1981, Aurora High School graduated more students than ever, with a very high number enrolled in college or trade schools. Also, in 1981 Aurora High School had the lowest dropout rate of any continuation school in California. That same year Aurora High School, one of over five hundred such schools in California, was named by the State Department of Education the number one continuation high school.

If you asked most people in the Imperial Valley if they'd heard of Aurora High School, their reply would be something like, "Isn't that the school that was burned to the ground?" And they'd be right, because they read the newspaper and watched the news.

In 1981, no one would write a news story about a principal who took a boy fishing, a boy who later became a school principal himself... and who then taught other boys to fish.

I know I probably should read the newspaper. My only defense is a simple: I have better things to do with my time.

There's one more story related to this incident that never made the news at all. The boy who'd tossed the lit cigarette lighter onto the puddle of gas from the full gas can that was tossed through the school's library window, sat with his wife and new baby in the courtroom to receive sentencing. The judge explained that the boy's family had paid the thousand dollar deductible on the school's fire insurance and now it was time to determine his actual punishment for the crime. To my surprise the judge addressed me. "Mr. Peake?"

He said that since my staff and students bore the brunt of the problems caused by this fire, he would like me to suggest a proper punishment. I respectfully addressed the judge explaining that I was neither a lawyer nor a policemen, I was an educator. That meant that I always looked more for what could be learned than the punishment. I told the judge that the learnings and blessings that came from this fire were profound. I only wished that this boy could also learn from this. He had mentioned in his testimony he had been taking care of an elderly grandmother. What if he could experience the deep experience of true service with many elderly people, people who have no one to visit them?

The judge sentenced the boy to three years of service in a convalescent hospital. I hope the young man found the true blessing in that.

13

ON BELAY

The delicate balance of mentoring someone is not creating them in your
own image, but giving them the opportunity to create themselves.

-Steven Spielberg

Do you belong? To a club, a family, a work group, a group of friends, a country, a Higher Power? Have you seen people who you suspect feel like they belong to nothing, to no one? My guess is you probably can think of someone like this.

Psychologist Alfred Adler said the need to belong is the primary need out of which all other needs evolve. To be a part of something, to be connected to someone, some place, something, to feel we, too, are chosen.

High schools often address this need through clubs, after-school programs, tutoring, activities, sports—all opportunities to belong to something. Yet there are some kids who separate from all of that. They join gangs, withdraw into drugs, try unprotected sex.

As the principal of a school for high-risk teens for over twenty years, I saw literally thousands of kids who did not join in the regular high school activities, who did not, as someone perceived it, *belong* in regular high school. Our school explored ways of addressing this important question: How do we make kids feel that they belong?

One thing we did was make those after-school organizations part of the curriculum. Chess club, soccer team, mixed girls and boys softball team, basketball team, Outward Bound teams.

I found a component of the rock-climbing adventure of Outward Bound that illustrates this need for connection; the belay line. In climbing rock faces, you have a belay line at the top looped around a fastened-down carabiner. One end of the line is held by your belay partner, while the other is fastened to a belt on your harness. As you climb, you risk moves you didn't think you could do. But you have your partner below to stop your fall, so you can try another choice if you get into trouble.

The power of this relationship came to me when I was on a rock face, looking for a hand-hold and not sure there was one. I looked down and saw that my partner on the ground, was Bullet, a big kid I had suspended from school weeks before. It was an existential moment. I made a leap for a questionable hand hold and slipped about a foot down before I felt the firm grasp of my belay partner. I swung a few feet into a perfect foothold. That led me to a sequence of holds all the way to the top. I heard Bullet's bull-like voice cheering as I reached the summit. When I got back down from that, he and I actually hugged.

Then there was Filomena. She was an extremely intelligent but under-achieving teenager who had just three connections; her dad, her best friend Perla, and her car. She graced our school with her presence occasionally. Most of the time she liked to cruise town in her pristine vintage pink Mustang convertible. She loved to show it off at the high school that had rejected her.

One afternoon, as that high school was letting out, Filomena was paying more attention to the people admiring her car than she was to her driving. She crashed head-on into a telephone pole, smashing her engine beyond repair. Her seatbelt assisted her in receiving only minor scrapes, but she had lost her car.

She called her dad, who was just beginning a night shift on his second job, and he was furious. Filomena wasn't even supposed to be there. She was supposed to be at our school. Filomena felt in that moment like she had lost her dad. Filomena went home, looked in the mirror, pulled out a razor blade, and slashed both wrists. As she watched the blood ooze out, she had one tiny thought. She picked up the phone, called her best friend—her last connection—and left a message on her answering machine.

"Hi, Perla. I just want you to know that I love you." Then, she hung up the phone.

Minutes later, Perla, alarmed by the call, raced over to her house, pounded on the front door and found it unlocked. She ran into Filomena's room and discovered the blood trail following it out the door leading to an outdoor shed. She opened the door, screamed, and called 911.

At two in the morning, I got a call from county mental health clinic. They let me know that Filomena was there and she was asking to talk to me. What she wanted to know was whether or not she was kicked out of school. I told her of course not.

Two weeks later, we selected Filomena to go with staff and nineteen other students to an Outward Bound trip to Joshua Tree, a national park full of climbing sights.

Filomena hooked onto the belay rope and climbed. She was a skinny little girl with orange hair and freckles everywhere, even on her ankles. Her belay partner was one of the female Outward Bound guides. Halfway up, her green eyes widened in panic. She could see no foothold, no handhold. She demanded that she be let down. The guide refused. She told Filomena "You can do this. We'll wait."

A half an hour later, she continued to scream. Besides all the swear words and curses to the guide's family, we heard, "I'm gonna die up here!"

Finally, when she figured out that the guide would wait for as long as it took, she lunged a hand out, and then a leg, and she climbed. When she got to the top, she threw her arms into the air and cheered. Her audience below also screamed in triumph. Filomena had reconnected with something bigger inside of herself.

Mentoring can be the belay for a child.

In the 1980's, the Rand Corporation did a study of thousands of high-risk children, children who, given their background, were not supposed to make it. Their profile led to jail, drugs, and/or early death. But they selected a hundred kids who made it, who defied the odds and became successful by anyone's measure. The researchers questioned these successful adults, extensively looking for the reasons they made it. They found one common link: Every one of them said that the one thing they had that made the difference was at least one adult in their life who was there for them no matter what.

Filomena had her dad. No matter how upset her dad was, he was always there for Filomena no matter what. Now she also had teammates who cheered her on. Plus, she had found a very special inner strength, which I believe comes from a bigger connection.

Which end of the belay line have you been on? I'll bet both. Remember those special people who held the other end of your rope and hollered up to you, "On Belay. Climb on!"

Take a moment, thank them, and climb on!

14

HANDS

The best way to find yourself is to lose yourself in the service of others.

-Mahatma Gandhi

The handshake is an exchange of energy between two people, declaring we are together in this moment, acknowledging each other. Hands that wave hello. Hands that wave goodbye. Hands.

Think about the doors they've opened in your world, the loved ones they have held, the work they have done. They have served you well, and they have served others.

When my son Robert was seven, I would take his small hand and cross the street to visit the convalescent hospital on Saturday mornings. We'd hang out with the residents, especially the ones who rarely had visitors. The nurses had told us about a resident named Bud who was from Oklahoma and who never received visitors…and, he was a fisherman. The first time we walked into Bud's room I asked, "They biting, Bud?"

"That look like a fishing pole?" He nodded at his walker.

"I got poles," I said. "Want to go fishing?" Robert looked at me like I'd finally gone off the deep end.

"Huh?" Bud was lost.

"You do know how to fish, don't you?"

He broke into a brown-toothed grin. "Sure, I wouldn't mind drowning a few worms before I head on to better things."

"How about next Thursday after work?"

The Imperial Valley thrived on canals, which were full of catfish and bass if you knew where to look. Robert and I spent the next five days catching fish all over the Valley, taking them all to the same small fishing hole, and releasing them there. I think we released about sixty fish in a fishing hole about the size of a small living room.

Thursday afternoon, after work and school, Robert and I picked Bud up in my van. Once his walker was folded and he was buckled in, we were off. As we approached a mini mart, Bud reached over and tapped me on the shoulder.

"Say Pat, I'm a little short on my chaw." He nodded at the place.

"Sure, Bud." I pulled over.

As I got out of the van, he said, "Say Pat, been a long, long time since I've had a cold one."

I stared at him. "What brand?"

He gave me that grin again. "Guess."

I brought Bud his tobacco chaw and a beer with the same nickname as his.

Robert and I got to that fishing hole, propped him up in a lawn chair, stuck a pole in his hand, and set his beer beside him. He held his pole in two gnarly hands for better grip. No more than ten seconds later, Bud hoisted his first catfish onto the bank.

"There ya' go." He suppressed his grin, trying to act like this was just normal in the life of a real fisherman.

Robert and I figured that during his hoisting in one fish after another, he took no more than three sips of beer, but they were important sips.

"Excuse me, boys." He stood and grabbed his walker. "This fisherman's got to go shake hands with the governor."

When Bud returned with his walker from the eucalyptus tree that served as his "governor's restroom," Robert and I just looked at each other and then back at Bud's wet pants. The best part came last. Bud put down his pole, took a chunk of chaw, and just sat. His eyes gleamed in the gold hues of the sunset. I'll never forget that special look in Bud's eyes. He was fishing.

We got back to the home after dark. The nurses pitched a fit. Apparently, Bud had forgotten to sign himself out.

Once they calmed down, one of them asked the right question, "How many did you catch, Bud?"

"Don't know."

"Why not?"

"Lost count." And he flashed that grin again.

A couple of days later, I felt a need to visit Bud by myself. I'd heard he'd been moved to Room

27 down the hall by the back door. That was the room where they put patients who either were headed for the hospital or in the process of "passing on to better things," as Bud put it.

I could hear Bud moaning from clear down the hall. I entered his room.

"Pat!"

"Yeah, Bud."

"Pat, I got a powerful hurt. You think you could see your way clear to a back rub?"

"Why, Bud," I said. "Next to fishing, it's one of my best skills."

I rubbed my hands together to warm them up. Bud turned to his side and I placed my hands on Bud's back. For a few minutes we talked about the fish he'd caught and after a bit, he became quiet.

The light in that hospital room seemed to brighten. A deep peace settled inside me, and I felt a big presence. And Bud...he appeared to be glowing. Some reading this, I am certain, know of this moment; the moment when all the pain of life, all the ups and downs, the wins and losses, are let go and all that's left is that Light, that

Light that was always in there, that Light that is here, right now. When I lifted my hands from his back, I knew that my friend had passed on to a whole new kind of fishing hole.

I put my hands together and bowed to my friend.

Thanks Bud. Thanks for a mighty fine fishing trip, and all that came with it.

Hands.

15

FEAR

*We can easily forgive a child who
is afraid of the dark;
The real tragedy of life is when we
are afraid of the light.*

-Plato

What are you afraid of?

Ever heard that question before? It's sometimes followed by a comment that is neither wanted, nor helpful.

"It's only..."

It's only water. It's only a spider. It's only a speech.

Many years ago, *pure fear* walked into my continuation high school office dressed in a white blouse, tennis shoes and a pleated schoolgirl uniform skirt. Her face was gaunt, eyes deep set, skin pale, her arms just the diameter of broomsticks. She looked like a photo of a Jewish prisoner who'd survived a concentration camp, except that Elena had no smile. She was still in the camp. She looked at me like I was her executioner.

I was asked to counsel Elena. Although she was in another school, the parents believed I might be able to help their daughter with her anorexia. I reminded them I was a school counselor, not a therapist. They said they just wanted to see if I could get her to talk a bit. I was relieved to hear she was seeing a doctor regularly for treatment and medical support. They asked me for emotional support. I agreed to do what I could, but with one condition. For every session with Elena, there would be another session with just her mom. In addition, there would be at least a couple sessions Elena, Mom and her very busy dad.

In our first meeting, Elena and I said very little. Some words triggered her into cringing and soon became forbidden for me to use. Words like *food*, *eat* and worst of all, *diet*. After some time, she began to share a little about herself. She had been a cheerleader, a top student, and popular. Her light had shined brightly. That's when the anorexia hit, and all that fell away, along with her weight.

At the very end of our session I asked her the question. "What are you afraid of?"

She stared at me with those deep-set penetrating brown eyes, licked her dry lips and said, "Being fat! Mr. Peake, when I look in the mirror, I see a *fat* girl." The fear in her eyes shined like a captured wild animal.

In her mom's first session, the robust lady came in the door smiling and talking. She kept it up through most of our session. Finally, she gave me an opening by asking, "What's wrong with her?"

"She's afraid of getting fat."

"What? That's ridiculous! You've seen her. Afraid? Give me a break!"

Then I asked Mom, "What are you afraid of?"

"What?"

"Surely, you have a fear of something."

She paused, thought a moment, and then actually cringed. "Snakes!"

"You mean," I nodded my head very slightly up and down looking at an empty spot on the couch. "If there were a snake on the couch beside you right now…"

"Stop!" She jumped to her feet.

"But you see, Mom, nothing's there."

She sat back down nervously. I said no more about it, but from that moment on she spoke only with compassion for her daughter's fear. In future sessions, a curious thing happened. Any time she would go into judgment about Elena, I would make that little nod and instantly, unconsciously, she would return to her compassion.

In my talks with Elena, we discovered that her fear started in elementary school with some painful events. Although her anorexia didn't strike until puberty, the triggers for the disease developed early on. In our talks, when she would share a painful childhood memory, I would ask her to put her hand on her stomach and comfort the younger self inside. She would say, "It's okay, little one. We're going to be just fine."

She would become calm.

While I am certain that our time together didn't "cure" Elena, that was okay. I felt honored to be let into her world, and I was impressed with her courage. I was just as impressed with her parents. Through their deep love for their girl, they learned to provide an even more nurturing, compassionate home. I'm sure that other professionals gave Elena the additional support she needed.

Some years later, I visited my old school district's opening day for employees. I saw her there. She was the new second grade teacher, and she looked beautiful. I knew that she probably still had to take a breath and muster a "thank you" when someone complimented her on how good she looked. I knew that the anorexia didn't just leave, it was managed. In fact, I didn't approach her because I was pretty certain that I represented a painful time in her life. Or was that just my *own* irrational fear?

I imagined one of Elena's second-graders listening to their new teacher when they felt hurt or afraid. Their teacher would probably say, "It's okay, little one. You're going to be just fine."

Sometimes, I find myself moving into my own secret fear, the fear that I will shine too brightly, and be condemned for it. I put myself in the prison of my own self-judgment. But then I remember Elena and I touch my stomach and I also say, "It's okay little one. You're going to be just fine."

16

THE BEST CUP OF COFFEE EVER

I wanna be loved by you, just you-ooo-ooo.
Boop boop be doop.

-Betty Boop

Betty Boop did not play chess. But Daniella—who also had huge brown eyes, short black hair, and a round-faced smile—did play chess. Her beauty and the fact that she barely spoke English added to the paradox. At first, I must admit, I figured she came across the border to our continuation high school simply looking to marry and get her citizenship.

At seventeen and only in the U.S. for a few months, she had about the equivalent of a fifth grade education. She joined the chess club, I assumed, because she found out there were only boys in it. Still, she seemed serious about school.

The guys soon discovered that she was more than just a test of their hormones. Daniella earned a coveted position as fourth board on our chess team. She wasn't a go-for-the-jugular aggressive player. She loved complicated situations in the middle game and making her opponent squirm. In a sweet voice and with an innocent smile, she would say, "Tu movida," reminding them that it was their move. She timed her comment to when her opponent looked confused by an unorthodox move she'd made. "Tu movida." They feared a trap. Frequently, it was enough to prompt the opponent into an overly reactive blunder. She would take the match.

There was one match I'll never forget. Our tiny high school for high-risk teens was set for a chess competition with Central High, a school of 2,000 students. In the first round, Daniella was paired with their first board, the district attorney's son. The boy had a national ranking. That match between Daniella and this young man was unforgettable. It wasn't the outcome. It was the expressions on their faces. It was also the trip to the match. But most of all, it was a cup of coffee.

Daniella gave me unique directions on how to get to her mother's house in Mexicali, Mexico that Saturday morning of the big match. Although she lived with her aunt in the U.S., Daniella visited her mom on the weekends. When the narrow, paved road turned to dirt, I knew I was on course. When I saw the goats in the road, I relaxed. She told me I would see goats. I knew I was almost there. I turned right at the huge, solitary salt cedar tree to the three "houses." Hers was the one on the left. It was four adobe walls with a tin roof on top and various spaces in it for a couple of doorways and windows.

I parked by an old rusty pickup and a burro. Three sparkly-eyed munchkins hurried into the doorway and out came Daniella beaming. "Hola, Mr. Peake! Come in and meet my mom."

As I came through the door, two chickens fluttered across the hard-packed mud floor and disappeared behind a blanket. The colorful cloth hung across the middle of the house to break it into two rooms.

Her mom was a surprisingly slight woman when compared to her round-cheeked daughter. Her heart, however, was big. She beamed as she shook my hand and asked me to please sit for a cup of coffee. It wasn't a question. It was a privilege.

Daniella, holding a white blouse fresh from the clothesline, snatched the flat iron sitting on top of the wood-burning stove, and disappeared behind the blanket. Three pairs of brown eyes smiled at me from its edge. I was escorted to an old lawn chair, the seat of honor.

Mom boiled water on the stove in a used coffee can. She scooped three spoons of ground coffee into the boiling water. After a few minutes she lifted the can off with a towel. She took a metal cup and filled it with water from a plastic bottle of commercial water. I was comforted by the water source being a U.S. mountain resort. She added the cool water to the boiled coffee and set down the empty cup. With two hands wrapped in the towel, she tilted the pan and the dark brown liquid streamed in. The cup handle was a bit hot. but I knew I was expected to sit there and drink her offering. It was good. It was real coffee. I could feel nerve endings perk up all over my body as the warm liquid flowed down my throat and warmed my stomach. I smiled. I usually like something in mine, but the love she put in this coffee you can't find in most places.

Mom told me what a good girl her daughter was and thanked me for all the education I was providing her. She looked me in the eye, watching my reaction to her words to see if I knew what she meant. I did. Her daughter was going to make it in the States and have a fine life. It was clear to both of us that this would happen. I thanked Mom for the coffee.

Daniela and I were silent in the car the entire hour it took to get to the chess match. Her big eyes seemed to get even bigger when we pulled up to the large, modern "American High School." The DA's son was waiting for her.

The vivid picture that stuck in my heart was of the stunned look on the face of the DA's son in the middle of the match. He was examining Daniela's beautiful face as she pondered the board. She suddenly looked up with large, brown, smiling eyes, and confidently pushed her queen one square forward. "Tu movida."

It was enough to distract the young man into making a weak move. For a while, all those not playing were gathered around her board. She'd gained the advantage and fought hard for the next half hour, but in the end, his mind overcame his hormones, and he managed a win. However, I believe that, this boy will remember the girl who extended her hand across the chessboard with the words, "Nice game."

Five years later, I was having lunch with my teachers at an upscale restaurant on the edge of town. Daniella was our waitress. We found out she was working her way through college. Her eyes sparkled like the diamond on her ring finger.

"Coffee." I smiled. "Although, it won't be as good as your mom's."

Her brown eyes brightened, and, in excellent English, she said, "Nothing is as good as my Mama's coffee, Mr. Peake. You know that."

17

INVISIBLE

*Courage is what it takes to stand up
and speak;
Courage is also what it takes to sit down
and listen.*

-Winston Churchill

Have you ever felt invisible? Like nobody even sees you when it comes times to choose sides for the big game?

For many years when I ran the continuation high school, I witnessed teens find unusual ways to make themselves visible; with drug use, pregnancy, violence, graffiti, and so on.

Then there was Alfonso who came to our school to make himself *invisible.*

He sat there in the chair in front of my desk, slouching down low, staring at his own shoes, mumbling his answers, never making eye contact.

One thing broke through his cloak of invisibility was basketball. He played every lunch hour. But even on the court Alfonso tried to keep himself invisible. He never called for the ball or made eye contact with his teammates. He just quietly slipped into an open spot.

When I played, I made sure Alfonso got the ball because it was like dropping a quarter into a machine. Automatic. He'd catch it, look over his shoulder, turn, and leap, shooting a perfect Kobe Bryant fadeaway jump shot. *Swish!*

Our school had a unique graduation requirement, one that would challenge Alfonso's invisibility. Every senior was required to design and perform a meaningful service project and present the project to a panel of adults from the community at the end of the school year. Another unique requirement of our school was punctuality, being on time for whatever you've committed to do. If a student was late to school, he or she was sent home to return with an adult advocate to chat with me about what message being late sends.

So when Alfonso was late for his own project presentation, I shook my head. I'd heard that Alfonso had a solid project and I was looking forward to hearing about it as I sat with his panel. Ten minutes later, Alfonso didn't show. Twenty minutes, still no Alfonso. I was apologizing to the panel and explained that Alfonso had forfeited his right to graduation, just as Alfonso walked through the door. He and his friend carried a large chest of drawers.

For the first time ever, Alfonso made eye contact with me. "Peake," he said, "I know I'm late and I don't graduate." He took a deep breath and let it out. "But I want to present my project anyway."

"Okay." I sat down and did my best to let go of my skepticism. We'd taught students that how we listen to someone is at least as important as what they say. It was time to practice it.

He stood there looking at his feet and I couldn't help it. I thought, *oh boy, here we go again.*

But then he looked up, placing a hand on the dresser. "My dad and me, we made this dresser for my grandma. My grandma asked me if I would make a dresser for her. But I know why. See, she knew that my dad and me, we never talked. I hardly ever saw my dad. He worked long hours driving a truck for his company. And when he got home he'd grab a beer and head for the garage where he worked on his wood. No one was allowed in there. So I asked him, Dad, will you help me make a dresser for grandma? To my shock he said 'yes.' We spent many nights, very late, working on the wood. He showed me the tools and how to use them and we talked a lot, about everything. He even showed me how he did this fine design work on the front of the drawers, but he said I wasn't quite ready for that yet."

Alfonso pushed the dresser closer to us. The surface of each drawer was chiseled a little deeper around a design of a leafed grapevine with a bunch of grapes hanging down. "See, my grandma used to work in the grapes when she was young and loved to swipe a few. She said she was making sure they were sweet enough."

Alfonso took a deep breath. "Three nights ago, my dad stopped on the freeway and got out of his truck to check a blowout. A car hit and killed him."

In the long pause that followed, I wondered if he would be able to go on.

"So…" Alfonso let out that breath, placing a hand on top of the dresser. He brought his other hand down pointing at the face of each of the lower three drawers… "My dad, he did the design on these. But I…I did this one." He touched the top drawer.

"See, I watched my dad very closely when he did this and listened to every word, every word he said, and I learned. And I did this drawer." He moved his hand over the design. It seemed to steady him. "And that is my project." He made eye contact with each panel member.

"I am late, because I just arrived from my father's funeral."

I can't think of anyone who'd made themselves more visible than Alfonso did at that moment. I could only muster a handshake and two words, "Congratulations, graduate."

Have you ever felt invisible? I know I have. But sometimes we all need to stand up, to tell our story, like Alfonso did.

18

UNFINISHED BUSINESS
(For Dick)

Now I know what a ghost is.
Unfinished business, that's what.

-Salman Rushdie

Suppose, for a minute that you are going on a long trip, leaving all your loved ones, all your friends, all the people with whom you worked, laughed, and played. You don't know when you will be back, if at all. Anything you need to do or say before you leave?

Do you have unfinished business?

For several years, after Dick Miller's death, I got this pain in my chest the last week of school. I called it the "Dick Miller Grip." The first year it clutched my chest I actually went to a doctor to check my heart. I had low cholesterol and triglycerides, great blood pressure, and I was a treadmill long-distance champion. The doctor looked up at me from the report. "Did something happen to you in the past, say around this time of year?"

The memory of Dick Miller hit me like a punch knocking the wind out of me. I gasped for air.

A year before, Dick, a retired chief petty officer, came to our school from the Navy. When I interviewed him for the teaching job, he said he wanted to share the world he had seen across three oceans with these teens who had never been out of the Imperial Valley. He taught social studies.

Dick had a way of teasing even the most difficult teen into learning something about the world he'd traveled. He'd say to the frowning boy, "You know, you've got a face only your mother could love." But he delivered it with such joy that the kid would just break into a grin.

I've got a classic photo of Dick etched in my mind. There he is after barbequing all day for a school fundraiser, floppy Budweiser hat on his nearly bald head, cigarette in one hand and a Styrofoam cup of black coffee in the other, looking at me like he's about to make a wisecrack.

His wife was his best friend, and they did everything together. The burden on Dick's shoulders was his three daughters. He said they grew up pretty much rudderless and resentful that he was never there when they needed him. He'd been deployed to all parts of the world.

On the last Monday of the school year, Dick came to my office with a bright light gleaming in his eyes. He sat on the couch and told me about the Catholic Church's Marriage Encounter he'd attended with his wife. He told me how he rediscovered his love for his high school sweetheart. But what really lit him up was that he wrote three love letters, as he called them. He wrote a love letter to each of his daughters, pouring his heart out to them, telling them how proud he was of them, asking for their forgiveness, and talking about things that had remained unspoken. The gleam in his eyes glazed with tears.

"I put them in the mail this morning." He handed me his grades for the year and marched to his classroom, face hidden in a magazine he'd grabbed off the rack.

An hour later, I walked down the halls and passed Dick's empty room during his prep period.

I spotted him slumped to the floor behind his desk. I called for help to some boys in the hall, and we carried him over to the hospital across the street. The emergency team tried to bring him back. Those same boys and I would carry him again later...in a casket.

I learned why they say you need to have everyone sit down before delivering tragic news. Dick's wife arrived at the hospital steps and, when I told her, she passed out in my arms. It had been a very long day for everyone, but hers would seem like an eternity.

Toward the end of that day, after everyone had gone home, I sat in that emergency room by myself. Twilight filtered through the windows in orange patches, giving the place an otherworldly feel. The room smelled antiseptic. As I stared at the sheet, lumped with Dick's body under it on a steel gurney, I heard a voice. Dick's voice. But it wasn't coming from the gurney. It came from the far, top right-hand corner of the room.

"It's okay, Pat. It really is okay. I'm fine. I'm more than fine. Much more."

Dick had finished his unfinished business.

I wish I could say the same. For several years after, at the end of each school year, I would still get those chest pains. Doctors assured me they had no physical cause. I knew the source of the pains. I had unfinished business with my dad. He too died of a sudden heart attack. But that's another story…

19

MY FATHER'S WISH

...greater is he that is in you,
than he that is in the world.

-John 4:4

Do you ever find yourself holding a conversation with a person who has been dead for quite some time? I mean, a long conversation, one that ends with, "I wish you were here."

When I am having one of these conversations, I'm usually fishing... and talking to my dad.

There is one message I wish that I could have delivered to my father in person. It has to do with God. Dad was a spiritual man. He read a portion of the great spiritual teachings every morning for as long as he was my dad. He spent time each evening thanking God for his blessings.

He'd determined that he wanted only one thing for his children. He revealed to me what that was one day in a special talk we had. That talk actually came on one of the hardest days of my life, the day I found out I had flunked out of college. That day I had to tell my dad I'd wasted his hard-earned tuition money. I'd received four F's and a C- in History of the English Language, a class I never wanted to take again.

I sat in the living room with him and watched his face as he took in the news. I told him I planned to take a year off, travel, and then see if I could re-enter college. He must have felt some disappointment, but it didn't show. He looked me right in my twenty-year-old eyes. "Son, it's okay. Whatever you do with your life is fine with me. Actually, I only want one thing for you, just one. The rest will take care of itself. I want you to find God."

I knew *God* was important to Dad, just not *how* important. I remembered a time etched in my heart when he showed us one place to find Him. He took my brother Chris and me on the vacation of a lifetime; canoeing, camping, and fishing on the island-filled lakes of Minnesota and Canada for two weeks. It was a dream come true for a sixteen-year-old boy and his thirteen-year-old brother. We camped on a pine-filled island, about the size of a small parking lot.

That first evening, Dad called us over to this big, flat rock looking out at a smooth mirror of water reflecting the last golden strand of sunset. The loons added their eerie song. Dad crouched on that rock, his big nose silhouetted, bald spots of a receding hairline shining from the shimmering water, his whole being still, reverent. To me, he looked like a giant poised there, yet I was a good five inches taller. We were in awe of this man. I tried to say something, but my dad put out his hand for us to remain silent. Several minutes later, with the gold light of the setting sun gleaming in his eyes, Dad arced his arm across the scene and said, "This, boys, is God."

Amid the bumps and bruises, wins and losses of life, we all went our separate ways as adults. Chris was very angry with our dad for leaving our mom and moving to Colorado from Iowa. Dad didn't fare well. He ended up in a small office with few clients for his dental technician practice, paying his bills with credit cards and loans. The irony is that Chris also moved to Colorado and became a millionaire by starting a robotics company. I moved to another country... California.

We all received invitations to a wedding of my cousin, who had also moved to Colorado, and I became very excited. Here was a chance for my dad and brother and me to all be together, like on the island. But Chris was adamant. He was still not happy about our dad's life choices. I really listened, and I also heard the love he had for Dad under it. Still, I wanted us all there. Chris softened a bit.

"I'll go. But I won't talk to the man."

`The wedding service was outdoors with a backyard reception. After the ceremony, all the guests mingled there on the lawn, sipping drinks and nibbling on snacks. The scene reminded me of one of those classic soap opera moments. You know the one where the two main characters, my brother and my father, are back to back chatting with various friends and family, coming closer and closer until they bump into each other.

They turned and faced each other. After seconds of excruciating silence, Dad said to Chris, "I don't care what you think or what you say, I just want you to know one thing. I love you, son."

Seconds more of silence and my brother took Dad into his arms. All three of us were together again, like on the island.

In the next month, Chris helped Dad to get on his feet, pay his debts, and get a decent place to live. They spent time together, time I wished I had taken.

One night, several months later, I got a midnight phone call from Dad. He was so excited. He'd read the Bible cover to cover many times and he'd just found the few lines that he believed summarized the entire message of the book. He gave me chapter and verse. And he just had to make sure I would get this one sentence. He read it aloud.

"God is love and he who dwelleth in love dwelleth in God and God in him. John 4:16."

I was so touched by his words, but even more by his incredible joy. When he hung up, I went to my great-grandmother's Bible and re-read the words.

It was later that very night that my dad passed away of a heart attack. Chris found him in his apartment the next morning. They had made their peace.

But now I have some business to finish, to fulfill my father's wish. And it's not about the A's and B's in those classes I retook.

Dad, I did find Him. He's right here with me. He always was.

Thanks, Dad.

20

GRANDMA

If nothing is going well, call your grandmother.

-Italian Proverb

Besides your dog, who loves you unconditionally? For me, no question about it. It was Grandma Alice Brown. We called her "Brownie."

I was six-weeks old. My teenage father and my mother had eloped and Grandpa had banned them from the house. But I was born and Grandma Brownie really wanted to see me. My mom sneaked me over to her house while Grandpa was working. Grandma scooped me up in her soft, plump arms smiling down at me with sparkly brown eyes. She sang and cooed with me the whole day. We became fast friends.

Grandpa came home early from work that day and saw me. She told the story.

"He came in, looked down into your crib, and said, 'What's that?' And stalked away."

For the first time ever, Grandma confronted Grandpa. She went over to him, took his arm, and said, "Come back here." Standing beside him in front of my crib, she said, "That happens to be your grandson."

Grandpa looked at me. As he stood there studying my face, I broke into a big grin.

"That was the first time I ever saw tears come to that man's eyes." That's what Grandma told me.

Just six years after that, Grandpa passed. The blessing was that Grandma moved upstairs into our house. Having her up there was perfect, because my mom was an alcoholic, and my dad worked twelve hours a day.

Mom sometimes became angry when she drank, and when it got a little rough downstairs, I went upstairs. I remember sitting with my grandma and watching Kate Smith on Wednesday nights. She was a singer who looked a bit like my grandma. She sang her theme song, "When the Moon Comes Over the Mountain," like a bird. I would settle in for the show with Brownie, usually holding something sweet she had just baked. Without comment, when bumps and yelling erupted downstairs, she simply waddled to the TV and turned up the volume.

Grandma and I had this connection like nobody else. We played bridge, which is a game played with a partner. I always loved to have my grandma as my partner. When she and I were partners, we cleaned the table. We won because I understood every grunt, every groan, every roll of her eyes that my grandma used, which, of course, was illegal at the bridge table. But with us, we just knew. Nothing was planned.

"Mmm?"

Oh, she doesn't have any spades.

"Ahh."

Oh, she got some hearts.

Yes, I always had a pretty good idea of what Grandma held in her plump fingers. We won game after game.

Several years after I visited Grandma in Iowa for her eightieth birthday, I got the phone call at my school.

"Pat, your grandma's dying." With the news, came a request. "The family wants you to be the minister for her funeral."

In my family, being as dysfunctional as it was, aunts and uncles resented other aunts and uncles. My mom had passed on but mixed feelings about her still stirred the family pot. This uncle didn't speak to that uncle, and this cousin only talked to this aunt, yet they all would be at Grandma's funeral. They all loved her. And all the family somehow managed to accept me. Maybe the fact that I was a foreigner, a Californian, led them to believe I was neutral in the family dynamic…like Switzerland.

I needed time to consider the request. They told me she was holding on by a thread and could go anytime. I got in my car and started driving around the little town of Calexico in search of a place to collect my thoughts. Now, the local priest there was a good friend, but I drove north and ended up in the Methodist Church where the minister there was a basketball buddy.

I went into the church and I asked my friend, "Say Reverend Mike, could I borrow your church for a while? I need some time here."

"Sure," he said. "Mind if I say a prayer with you first."

"I would love that."

"Who's it for?"

"Grandma...and me."

So Mike sat beside me in the pews and said a prayer for us.

After, I sat silently for what must have been a good half hour, listening. I heard Grandma's voice inside of me.

"I can't go yet."

What, what did you say?

I can't go yet, because of your Aunt Linda. Aunt Linda took care of Brownie all those later years. She was as much a treasure in my life as my grandma. *I'm afraid that if I die, Aunt Linda will become an alcoholic like your mom. So I can't go yet.*

Okay, I whispered inside myself. *Want me to do the funeral?*

You know my answer to that. I could visualize her dark brown eyes twinkling. I was ready to bid six hearts.

I called up my family back in Iowa and told them I would do the funeral when the time came.

Almost a week later, I was attending a spiritual conference in, of all places, Las Vegas. Yes, indeed, God is everywhere. I woke up in our hotel room there at two in the morning. I couldn't go back to sleep, I felt anxious. Sitting in a comfortable chair, I said a prayer for Grandma, and became quiet inside. Minutes later, I heard my Grandma's voice.

"It's okay, Patric. Your Aunt Linda's all right. She's going to be just fine."

With that, I was able to go back to sleep. An hour later I received a phone call from my family.

"Pat, Grandma Brownie has just passed away."

The funeral was special. I saw my family together; my whole family, the family who used to all come over for Christmas dinner and all play penny-ante poker late into the night. Sadly, this funeral was the last time we all gathered.

Grandma was right. Aunt Linda's doing fine. I

recently, attended her eightieth birthday. All her grandchildren were there. I could see that they hold their grandma in the same special place in their heart that I hold mine.

There are certain people in our lives who live inside of us, who will live there forever. Whenever I find myself becoming a little down on myself, I call Grandma.

21

YOU WANT TO BE HAPPY?

It doesn't matter what the critics say,
I write what interests me in my own way.
I know they have to fill up the reviews
With what is called literary news.
And as my poems go by I hope you seize
On one or two that make you nod your head
As if you liked them. Poet Yeats once said
Of poetry and the critics' wailing wall.
"It's not a matter of literature at all."

-James Hearst

What stops your clock, makes time vanish, brings you to that place of peace inside that transcends all the troubles of the world?

It is in the very act of writing this story that I

go to that place where time does not exist, and peace does. People find this special place in a variety of ways; knitting, meditating, fishing, making music, fixing a car, creating art, cooking a special dish, having coffee with a dear friend.

As a freshman at the University of Northern Iowa, I thought I was supposed to become a rocket scientist. After all, the Russians had beaten us to space. But calculus was hard work and no fun and I was always under the law of the clock with homework.

My senior roommate, who was an English major, saw something in my freshman compositions and told me I had to meet Mr. James Hearst. The trouble was, to take his class in poetry writing, you had to be a junior and an English major. Fortunately, my roommate was also student body president and knew how to navigate college. He got me in the class as a freshman math major.

That poetry class met one night a week, for three hours, in Mr. Hearst's basement. Walking down the steps to the classroom, you couldn't miss that ramp instead of a rail that lowered a metal platform.

Picking a spot on the arm of one of the couches that arched around the teacher in the center, I was happy to be able to stretch my long legs in front of me. He sat in a wheelchair, doubled over, eyes shut, like he was taking a snooze. He had a grey-haired crew-cut, country plaid shirt, khaki slacks, legs crossed and slippers. A quadriplegic with just enough mobility to type with two fingers, one on each hand, he sat in silence. When the final student found a seat, he came alive. A fire burned gently in the fireplace, and its light glistened in Mr. Hearst's bright grey eyes.

He spoke, it seemed, to some internal guest, closing his eyes often to find the right word, but he also glanced up regularly, memorizing our faces. His words tasted to me like buttered cornbread doused in maple syrup. I was home. Not that place I grew up...the bigger *home,* inside me. Three hours were three minutes. I loved the man instantly.

Passing by his house a few blocks from University one day, I saw him through the side window of his home at his writing desk. With his eyes tightly shut, he banged on the side of his wheelchair struggling to corral some maverick metaphor. He made it look like hard work, but I just knew he was in his joy. As hard as he seemed to be on himself as he wrote, that was never the case with his students. The only words he had for us were words of encouragement. The closest he came to corrective feedback was, "See how great you did this over here? Do that over here."Mr. Hearst became a second dad to me. He believed in me and in my writing. More than that, I think he saw a light in me I couldn't yet see myself.

He took me for rides in his hand-driven, converted New York taxi cab. We would park in front of a tall cornfield and talk about the meaning of life, writing, girls and basketball. I was on the freshman team. He'd been a player in high school until he dived headfirst into an Iowa river and hit an underwater log, breaking his spine.

One morning, Merle, his caretaker/wife, was out shopping, and he invited me over to make him breakfast; a piece of toast, a sunny side up egg and a glass of orange juice. I felt honored.

I told him I wondered if I was ever going to be happy. My girlfriend had broken up with me. All the late nights spent with her and *not* with my school books, left me with failing grades. Back home, my mom's alcoholism was at a new low.

"How can I be happy, Mr. Hearst?"

He said something I didn't understand.

"Hell, Pat. You just want to be *happy* all your life?"

I was stunned. I couldn't wrap my mind around his words. I knew there was wisdom in them, but it was lost on my twenty-year-old mind. Then I looked up and realized I was talking to a quadriplegic man in a wheelchair, and I felt stupid for asking the question.

It seems to have taken me over fifty years to finally come to an understanding of what I think Mr. Hearst meant. I finally got it. Do I just want to be happy? Or do I want to write? To write with joy for the wins and compassion for the losses. To write about our human experience.

I remember one of the letters I received from him while I was in Mexico on my year-long journey after flunking out of college to discover the meaning of life. I had shared how I felt my life had been reduced to a dirty old car that I slept in with my feet out the window. He wrote:

Sometimes you have to get in the dirt in order to appreciate the clean. Keep going Pat. I find just getting up in the morning and doing what's ahead of you to do can be the greatest act of courage.

All I have left from Mr. Hearst are a few letters of support, a full-length black and white picture of him in his wheelchair and a vivid memory of his eyes seeing the best in me. For the world, he left about a thousand of his poems in many books.

As I sit here rewriting and polishing this piece, I glance down at my watch for the first time. It felt like about ten minutes. Actually it was hours.

What stops your clock?

22

THE BEST HAMBURGER EVER

If you ever have to support a
flagging conversation,
introduce the topic of eating.

-James Henry Leigh Hunt

Hamburger and French Fries. We all know them. Most of us at least have tried them. Many of us remember a time when we had the best hamburger ever. It wasn't just about the delicious juice dripping down our cheek, or the warm, golden-brown fry dipped in ketchup that we popped into our mouth. It was about so much more...

Here are two stories about two very different people, but each carry the same message. First, my son, Robert. By his senior year of high school, Robert was sporting a nose ring and blue hair and cruising around town on roller blades. The irony was, that when he went off to college at UC Berkeley, he lost the blue hair and the ring because he thought it made him look like everyone else. He did, however, become a vegan following his girlfriend's lifestyle, at least to a point. At Thanksgiving, it was tofu turkey. Yuck!

In his junior year, he came home from college for a break. We were shooting baskets on our driveway basketball court. His tall, trim body leapt and shot with joy, leaving his busy mind to rest for the moment. However, I thought his vegan life left him looking a little pale...and he seemed preoccupied.

He told me he was waiting for an important phone call from his girlfriend. He suspected that she might have developed a habit that, for him, was a deal breaker. It was a habit that is very common in Berkeley, California.

The phone call came, and he took it upstairs. After a long talk, he came back down and joined me on the court with a somber look on his face. I tossed him the basketball, and he shot it half-heartedly, missing the rim.

"What happened?" I asked.

"She said she's not going to stop just because her boyfriend doesn't like it." Robert bent over, picked up the ball, and rotated it in his hands. "So I told her, that's it. We're done." He tossed me the ball.

I just stayed quiet. I shot a layup and tossed the ball back to him.

He held the ball and just stood there a moment looking at the ground. Then he looked up at me and said, "Dad?"

"Yes."

"Let's go to Wendy's" He took a shot. *Swish!*

"Wendy's…as in the burger place?"

He nodded with a mischievous grin.

We ordered double, double beef! It was his first meat in two years. We savored these juicy treasures. Sitting there a good long while, we talked about the meaning of life, one French fry at a time and had the best hamburger ever… and then another.

As for the second story, it came after my time

at the continuation high school where I worked with some challenging teens and tough-looking kids, who were, after all, just kids. When I got the job running an elementary school in Ojai, California, I thought I'd said goodbye to all of that. Those innocent bright-eyed elementary students caught my heart.

One day my secretary buzzed me to let me know that a substitute teacher had locked horns with Brock McCullough, one of our more challenging fifth-graders. He had a great fifth-grade teacher who was making real progress with him. The sub, however, had ordered him to pick up a pencil she thought he'd dropped. The kid bent over the pencil but then refused. The sub lost it, and she pushed his head down "toward the floor." That was the story that got back to me.

I got up to hurry over to the classroom and rectify the situation just as we received another phone call, this time, from Brock's father. We had thought Mr. McCullough was in prison, but apparently he'd just gotten out…and somehow he got a call from his son. The secretary had to hold the receiver away from her ear. I could hear him clearly, standing a few feet from her desk.

"I'm coming over now! Heads will roll!"

I quickly handled the "situation" with the sub and returned to my office to intercept Mr. McCullough. I was in familiar territory. I'd learned how to deal with irate parents in my former job, the hard way.

Mr. McCullough burst into my office uninvited. He looked just like one of my old continuation students. Tattoos careened down his neck and all over his arms. A teardrop etched under one of his blazing eyes memorialized an incident at a bar in town: a murder, with Mr. McCullough's gun.

"You the bossman here?!" He pointed his finger like a pistol.

"Hello, Mr. McCullough." I extended my hand. "I'm Pat Peake, the principal."

He scoffed at my hand like it was slimy. "Where's that asshole teacher who bashed my kid's head into the floor. I'm gonna bash her head into the floor."

"Well, Mr. McCullough, she was a substitute teacher and she has left campus and won't be back..." I paused and looked into his dark, questioning, eyes and added "…ever."

"She better not if she wants to keep her face. Nobody roughs up my boy. Nobody."

I had the thought, *nobody, except maybe you.* But I knew better.

"Mr. McCullough, I think you're here because you really care about Brock."

"You're damned right I do!"

"Look." I hadn't shut the blinds. Kids were slowing down outside my window to get a view of what was going on. "I've got an idea. I missed lunch today. How about if you and I go get a bite to eat? My treat."

He paused and took a breath. "Yeah," he said. "I could eat."

Can you guess where I took him? That's right, Wendy's.

We had a hamburger, fries, and a soda at Wendy's, and we talked about the meaning of life. Mostly I listened. He talked about prison and how you never got to just kick back and be yourself. You always had to wear a mask, and the scarier it looked, the better. He leaned back in his chair and relaxed.

I will always remember the gleam in his eyes when he talked about how he didn't want his son to end up like him. After a long pause, Mr. McCullough put down his burger, looked around, and he said, "You know, it's been a really long time since I've been in a nice restaurant like this."

My son Robert married the real girl of his dreams, who does eat meat by the way, and moved to England. He lives a good life, has a great job, and has published several amazing books of poetry. He loves his wife and is doing well. I'm sad to say Mr. McCullough went back to prison and was knifed to death by fellow inmates. Maybe even harder for me to talk about is that, his son Brock was transferred to another school in another town. As a young teen he was involved in a murder, and may have ended up in the same prison as his dad.

But what I like to remember about each them, both Robert and Mr. McCullough, is a moment in time when we sat together and talked about the meaning of life, as we ate the best hamburger ever.

23

SHAME

We're often afraid of looking at our shadow because we want to avoid the shame or embarrassment that comes along with admitting mistakes.

-Marianne Williamson

Have you ever done something that you are so ashamed of that you've literally locked it away in your subconscious only to have it pop up right in front of your face at the worst possible moment? I have too.

That worst possible moment for me, is right now, writing this.

A short time ago, I awoke at four in the morning with a clear and vivid memory of an event from a long time ago.   It came with a directive:

You are to write about it and to speak about this to an audience. But not just any audience; to an audience with at least one gay man in it.

It was at college in the early sixties, my first time away from home. My senior roommate, who I'll call Frank, was known as what they call today, "a player." He introduced me to drinking, girls and poetry.

One weekend, I went with him to his small, Iowa hometown to hang out. Frank took me to a bar where he knew they would let in a nineteen-year-old if he just said he was twenty one. The music was loud. Frank danced and hit on several ladies. I sat and drank.

Having no luck with the ladies that night, Frank joined me at our table. As he tipped his beer, he spotted a man, mid-thirties, sitting alone, watching the people, like us.

"Check him out," Frank said. "He's looking at just the men."

"So?"

He frowned at my naivety. "Let's go have some

fun."

"May we join you?" Frank asked the man.

"Sure!" He looked pudgy, a little drunk and self-conscious, probably a salesman. His eyes fixed on me. "Can I buy you a drink?"

What followed were innuendos, comments about male anatomy, and finally an invitation for the two of us to go back with him to his motel.

Frank kicked me under the table and gave me a look that said to follow his lead. "Sure," he said. "We'll follow you in our car."

"We can go in mine and I can bring you back." He looked nervous.

"Your motel's on our way home."

"Okay."

We all went to the lobby to pick up our coats. The man took my coat from my hands and, before I realized what he was doing, he tried to help me put my coat on, wrapping his arms around me.

I felt a jolt of electricity shoot down my spine. I turned violently and punched him in the face. We got out of there. I don't remember much else. I just remember Frank laughing about it on the way home and me feeling like I'd just kicked a puppy.

There you have it. I'd forgotten how much shame I felt about that.

After completing a couple of advanced degrees, my life served me an opportunity to make amends for this incident. It almost felt like a homework assignment from God, from that time on. Working for a university, I found myself giving counsel to several gay men and lesbian women. I have been privy to the joy and the pain of their lives. I have actually tried to support a man who reminded me of that man in that bar. He was a good man, a well-educated man. A few years after our time together, this man ended up taking his own life.

Several gay men continue to be in my life and in my heart. This piece is for you guys as well.

I want to say to you that I apologize. I also want to apologize to myself for carrying around this shame for so long. I know that I am a good man and I know that I am human, and I think it's important that I remember both.

Still, I want to say the words again to all concerned. I apologize.

24

FISH AND BELL PEPPERS

Of late I appear to have reached a stage
when people who look old are only my age.

-Richard Armour

A few years ago, at a writer's conference, sitting at a large round table with ten other writers, I became aware that I was clearly the senior member at the table. Then a young woman turned to me and asked, "How would you like to die?"

I paused. I didn't think I looked *that* close.

My answer was simple. I gave it to her. But what I didn't tell her was the story that brought me to my answer… When my wife and I married, I wanted to show her how much I loved her by learning to like bell peppers. My wife wanted to show me how much she loved me by learning to like fishing.

In the bell pepper department, I have done well. I now love bell pepper and put it in about everything but ice cream.

In the fishing department, my wife did well too…for five years. One summer day, she made a perfect cast from our boat and hooked a beautiful, huge bass. It turned heads as she carried it on the docks. Strolling down the walkway, a foot shorter than me, brown hair fluttering in a gentle breeze, brown eyes hiding a smile behind a look that said, *"Oh this fish? No big deal."*

That night, I showed her how to clean and fillet that fish. We cooked in on the campfire and had a tasty dinner. Since she caught it, I insisted she have the bigger fillet.

"Where's the lemon?" she asked.

I was, at the time, clueless to the fact that my wife actually did not like the taste of fish.

In our tent, after the meal, she announced that she had caught her last fish. She was done with fishing. It was years later I found out from her that it was the cleaning of the fish and all the guts that turned her off to fishing.

However, a few years ago, we were celebrating our fortieth anniversary. We had the kids over for a Mexican dinner featuring my amazing salsa with its secret ingredient: bell pepper. My wife's anniversary card had a smaller plastic card inside. I was certain it was my traditional coffeehouse gift card.

But inside, in that little plastic holder was a fishing license, a fishing license with *her* name on it! My son and daughter smiled, enjoying their father's tears.

I announced, "This is the best anniversary present ever!" Little did I know how true those words were or why.

I didn't even mind the one stipulation she put on her fishing with me: Catch and release only.

A couple of weeks later, my amazing wife, decked out in fishing hat and pole in hand, followed me down the beach past a power plant to a trusted spot for surf fishing at low tide. The drainage stream we crossed from the plant was ankle deep.

Fishing was slow, so after a couple hours, we headed back to find a new spot. The tide had risen so now we were thigh-deep crossing the drainage stream that had widened. At the halfway point, we heard a siren from the power plant which signaled they were releasing waste water from the plant. Suddenly we were waist deep, *my* waist deep, in a raging torrent!

I braced myself sideways against the crush of water, but the force knocked the love of my life right off her feet. I grabbed her hand. I knew I was hurting her, but I wasn't about to loosen my grip. Her body lifted in the violent flow, parallel to the water, her feet pointing out to sea. Water crashed against her shoulders and face. The look of terror in her eyes is etched in my mind forever.

I had always thought that I had a fear of death. In that moment, I realized the real fear, the fear of having to say goodbye to my beloved for the last time. All my old ideas were washed away by one clear and unwavering thought.

If she goes, I go.

I held on, as they say, for dear life. I shuffled sideways, pulling her behind me. I slipped and felt the possibility of our death upon us; a truly sickening feeling. Not only was there that powerful release from the plant, there was a vicious riptide that day.

I managed to regain my footing. I moved slowly to the other side where her knees finally touched bottom and we crawled to dry sand. Lying on our backs, we thanked the bigger Hand that had held us.

You know, I still love bell peppers, but I have no need for my wife to fish. That day, I was given a gift; a gift much bigger than a fishing license. It was a gift of deep loving, of deep gratitude for another day with my beloved.

When I told my wife my answer to the writer's question, she said to me, "But what if I die first?"

"No worries," I said. "Because you see, my dear, in my heart I am always holding your hand."

How would I like to die?
Simple.
"Holding my wife's hand."

When, after a long pause, I gave my answer to that young woman at the table, she began to weep. I learned from her that, in her heart, she was holding the hand of her beloved, who had recently passed away.

I offer the same question as a gift to you. Really.

How would you like to die?

This question leads to another equally important question: "How would you like to live?"

25

A FAREWELL TO ROBERT

I will go on speaking to you as long as I live.

-Robert Peake

I bid Robert "welcome," seconds after his birth, gazing into his eyes, stunned by a brilliant light coming from within. He came to me on my birthday...our birthday.

Part of me knew that Robert was not really of this world. At five years old, he dictated his first original poem that read like a spiritual discourse. Another part of me knew, at his birth, that it was my job to make him familiar with the things in this world. I started right away.

At one day old, I stuck a rubber ball in his hand, told him it was a basketball, and taught him a hook shot. He used that shot as a teen in pick-up games as my teammate.

At two days old I stuck a chess knight in his tiny hand and taught him the Ruy Lopez opening. In high school, he became the top player on the chess team.

At three years old, we read to him from a Pop-Up Spider-Man book many times, at his request. In a few years, he was reading at an adult level. At twenty-three, he and I went together to the opening of the first *Spider-Man* movie and watched it together from the third row.

At age six, I brought him a computer. In a few years, *he* was teaching *me* programming code. After high school, he received a scholarship to Berkeley in computer science.

I took him fishing, camping and hiking. I was his assistant scoutmaster for Boy Scouts. The camping and hiking hooked him. The fishing did not.

One day, he asked me to take him hunting with his new BB gun. He wanted to see what it was like to shoot something. I took him to an asparagus field where red-winged blackbirds flocked. He picked out his prey, fired one shot, and down went the bird with a hole through its eye. That was his first and *last* hunting trip. Years ago, he wrote a poignant poem about it.

During a Spring Break from college, I feared that I might be saying farewell to Robert in a more permanent way. Late at night, he came into our bedroom buckled over in pain. We rushed him to the hospital for a *routine* appendectomy. As we sat down the hall from the operating room, one of the nurses stuck his head out the door and said to another nurse, too loudly, that Robert was not going to make it.

Robert had gone into anaphylactic shock in reaction to the anesthesia. His lungs filled with fluid. Doctors drained them and he was taken to intensive care to see if his mom and I could help him to stay in this world by encouraging him to breathe on his own, despite his incredible pain. We took shifts all night.

I visited the special room they had for loved ones; a spiritual room. I had a conversation with God. It was more like a request. That's where I became acutely aware that I was not in any way in charge of Robert's destiny. I went back to his room and took my shift in encouraging Robert to breathe on his own, which he eventually did.

Sometime later, I shared with Robert my epiphany from that experience. All my concerns, dreams and expectations for him boiled down to just one request. "Please," I said, "I'd just like you to keep breathing."

He seemed to be okay with that request and I am grateful.

Several years later, he experienced his own infant son's assisted breathing for just three days. I watched Robert cradling his son in his arms, as he left this world.

There are no words for describing the Light in that hospital room as Robert's son passed on, nor the grief that followed. Only poets seem to catch some particle of experiences like these. Robert spent the next several years becoming the poet who could put in words what Wordsworth called, "thoughts that lie too deep for tears."

He completed his MFA in poetry, and would share his poetry in many readings and magazines. He would publish several highly acclaimed books of poetry. All the while, he would maintain a great day job, and an abiding love for his wife and family.

But as I said earlier, Robert was not much for convention. He needed a challenge, and being married to a British girl, he loved England. One day he announced at dinner that he didn't know how, but they would be moving to the UK. When I bade Robert farewell a few weeks after his announcement, I remembered that "farewell" means "fare thee well in the world." The world I did my best to introduce him to. I would not be saying goodbye. In a poem to his deceased son, Robert writes in the last line, "I will go on speaking to you as long as I live."

Robert, I will go on speaking to you as long as I live. There simply is no way that you can ever leave me. Your light beams too brilliantly in my heart.

Keep breathing, son.

26

THE BEST DANCE

Some people don't believe in heroes,
but they haven't met my daughter.

-Patric Peake

What prompts a sixty-five-year-old man with two left feet to take up dance lessons? There can be only one answer: Love.

Twenty-nine years earlier, I watched Lisa come out of her mommy's tummy and into my life. I thanked God for my girl. Little did I know then that God had plans for her and me...and those plans included several dances. Our first dance. And the next dance. And the special ones after that.

There was trouble at her birth. Her breathing

wasn't right. Concern on doctors' faces translated into fear in our hearts. Her six-year-old brother Robert, my wife, Margaret, and I waited. We visited her incubator. Nurses struggled to find veins in her head for IVs to drip life-saving fluids into her.

She cried and cried. The only thing that seemed to calm her was her big brother's voice. He would talk to her, and she would stop crying to listen to him. It's been like that between them ever since.

We were told she would need to be helicoptered to a children's hospital for special treatment. We gathered around her to say goodbye until we could meet again at the new place. We prayed, we cried, and Robert talked to his sister.

We returned to my wife's room and waited. I picked up the phone. I called everyone I could think of to ask for prayers and good thoughts. Several spiritual groups began to pray for Lisa.

We were told the helicopter was on its way.

Five minutes later, the doctor came in with a strange look on his face. He studied our faces and he said, "Something happened in the last five minutes. She's okay. Everything checks. She can stay and go home with you tomorrow. We've sent the helicopter back."

Tears of relief filled my wife's eyes. Robert seemed unsurprised. I clenched my teeth and waited to see for myself if the doctor's words were completely true.

She did go home with her mom and breast fed voraciously. A few nights later, at two in the morning, she cried for milk. I took her from her crib and laid her beside her mom, who was still weak from the C-section. When Lisa finished, and I took her in my arms, she broke into tears. I whisked her off to her room to let her mom sleep.

Again, she cried and cried. I rocked her. I talked to her. Nothing worked. Desperate, I reached for a portable cassette player and headphones. I clicked on "We are Family." And Lisa and I had our first dance.

As we danced, I heard a voice inside my heart. My little girl's voice. She whispered to me, "It's all right, Daddy. I'm alive and I am all right. I really am okay. And I'm your little girl."

Then I cried and cried.

When the song was over, I looked at her face

through my tears. She was sound asleep; yet, I swear I could see a special little smile on her face.

It was the exact same smile I noticed on her face eight years later. My wife had a nighttime commitment with our son, and I was home with Lisa. She asked me to take her to the video store because there was a movie she wanted me to see with her.

We sat on the couch together. She pushed the remote and on came *Father of the Bride*. The tears started with the basketball scene. Then there's the father, dancing with his little girl.

And guess what? I cried and cried.

I looked over at Lisa. She had that special smile, the mischievous, loving smile. She said, "I knew you'd cry Daddy. I just knew it."

It seems like just a blink of an eye later she called me to tell me she was getting married.

So the dance lessons began. This father would be dancing once again with his little girl, with the bride. I knew then that Lisa knew, and Margaret knew, and Robert knew, that the man who held back the tears at her birth, would be unable to hold back anything that day.

But he would dance.

And we did. At the time, I thought it was the best dance. Actually, the "new" best dance of all would come several years later. Within a year, Lisa discovered that her husband was, let's say, "out of step," and she had to let go of that dance partner. But sometime later, she found her real partner, Hugo, who could not only take the lead, but could also follow, and listen and love. They asked me to marry them. I was honored.

It wasn't a dance exactly, it was a processional. I was so proud and filled with joy as I marched down the center aisle with my beautiful daughter on my arm. We arrived at the altar. I turned and stood between them...and I didn't cry. Ministers have a job to do that precludes tears.

But I must say, that my *favorite* dance of all (to date) is a dance I had with Lisa and Hugo's son, my grandson, Luca. During a time I was babysitting, he was having trouble going down for his nap. I remembered my first dance with Lisa. I took him in my arms, put his head on my shoulder and we danced and danced. This time I sang.

"This old man, he played one, he played knick knack on my drum, with a knick, knack paddy wack, give your dog a bone, this old man came rolling home. This old man..."

A few days later, I got a text from Lisa:

So Luca starts singing "this old man" while falling asleep. Then he stops nursing and says "Pat! Pat!"

I'll bet that as Lisa texted that to me, she had that special smile on her face, the same one she had at the end of our first dance.

27

MY IRISH HOME

Too-ra-loo-ra-loo-ral,
Too-ra-loo-ra-li,
Too-ra-loo-ra-loo-ral,
Hush now don't you cry!
Too-ra-loo-ra-loo-ral,
Too-ra-loo-ra-li,
Too-ra-loo-ra-loo-ral,
That's an Irish lullaby.

-James Royce Shannon

An early childhood memory revisits me on odd occasions. Like now. It feels like a dream, but it's not. I am two or three years old in my bed. An angel, blonde hair glistening in the moonlight, sits beside me and sings me that song. An Irish angel, born of Irish heritage, on St. Patrick's Day.

My mother.

My first trip to Ireland was a journey home. Everything felt familiar. My son Robert, daughter-in-law Val, and my beloved Margaret all cruised by miles and miles of stone fences, surrounded fields of shallow topsoil, displaying Ireland's many brilliant shades of green.

The stone remnants of the Norman conquest broke the pastoral horizon with aging castles and crumbling fortress walls which, eventually, resulted in many Normans becoming Irish themselves. The Aran Islands protected the abbeys where the Irish monks saved civilization, scribing the great literature of the world, including the works of St. Patrick.

This man, consigned to Ireland on a slave ship to serve as a shepherd, offered compassion and connection to a spiritual world that had been about servitude and punishment. St. Patrick's Breastplate Prayer now hangs on the wall in front of my desk.

These words from that prayer visit me often: *Christ with me, Christ before me, Christ behind me. Christ in me.*

While this tale stirred me, nothing stirred me more than the people themselves. Thomas Cahill, in his book on *How the Irish Saved Civilization* talks about three qualities of the Irish: Their honesty, their generosity, and their courage. I would add to these, their ability to engage in conversation with anyone, their sense of humor, and their skill in telling a colorful, slightly embellished story. In chatting with the Irish from farm to coffee shop, from pub to riverbank, I found myself with kindred spirits. I was home.

There was my first day in Ireland. I trudged back to the home we rented carrying three full bags of groceries. An Irish woman with her daughter pulled her car up beside me and offered me a ride, along with a lovely chat. There was The Nook, a tiny coffee shop in Athenry with delicious coffee and delightful visitors of all ages. The owner told us this little shop and the floor above it was once the home of the Rabbit family. All twelve of them.

Even when I returned to England, the Irish found me. Fishing on the river Lea in

Wheathampstead, I wasn't having much luck. A smiling man came up to me and I instantly recognized two things about him. He was a fisherman, and he was Irish.

"Any luck?"

"Well," I said. "Not until just now." I yanked on a large fish, which I maneuvered up the stone wall, gently removed the hook, and returned the big fellow to the river.

He grinned. "Part Irish?"

I nodded. "Name's Pat.

He, indeed, was a fisherman. He even showed me his special fishing license with a picture of a carp on it. Now carp in the U.S. are considered a trash fish. He must have caught my look, because Mike reminded me of the catch-and-release laws of England. "So the flavor of the fish matters not." His biggest so far was a 40-pounder. At that point, I did what any good Irish lad would do, and I gave him my secret carp bait formula. You melt pig lard and hard cheese in a pan. Add garlic, mustard and ketchup. Take crust-less white bread and soak it in the potion. Let it cool and wad it into a dough ball. The carp go crazy over it. I knew, that with this offering, I had changed Mike's life forever, as he and all his Irish heritage, had changed mine.

Too-ra-loo-ra-loo-ral,
And now that childhood lullaby is with me.
Too-ra-loo-ra-li,
It is before me.
Too-ra-loo-ra-loo-ral,
It is behind me.
That's an Irish Lullaby.
It is in me.
Thanks, Mom.

28

BEFORE I WAKE

Now I lay me down to sleep,
I pray the Lord my soul to keep,
if I should die before I wake,
I pray the Lord my soul to take.
Amen

-Christian child's prayer-

My dad would sit on the edge of my bed, have me fold my hands, close my eyes, and say those words. Many times, when we would get to the part about "if I should die," I would feel fear wrapping its fingers around my throat. If I should die! The rest of it didn't help much. "I pray the Lord my soul to take." What did that mean? I was afraid to ask my dad because it seemed so important to him.

Dad was a loving man, and I am quite certain his devotion to having me say my prayers with him was out of love. I'll also bet my prayers gave *him* comfort. He often worked very late, so prayer time was special.

As a small child, another thing I remember was a game we kids played called Tiddlywinks. With a plastic squidger about the size of a nickel we tried to flip a plastic wink about the size of a dime into the pot by pressing down hard on the edge of the piece. When someone finally flipped one into the pot, we would all laugh and cheer and pat the guy with the squidger on the back. What joy!

Years later, these two events from my childhood came together in one remarkable experience. My wife's dad Bill was dying of Amyloidosis. I spent his last thirty-six days with him.

Bill, a beloved psychiatrist in a small New Mexico town. Bill, the gardener and builder of fish ponds. Bill, the father who always called his daughter, the teacher, on the first day of school and who called her once a week thereafter to check on the progress of the more troubled kids. Bill, my good friend. These were his last days. He had chosen the DNR and I had chosen to be Bill's care provider along this journey.

During those thirty-six days, I watched Bill's body dwindle while his spirit expanded. I began reevaluating what was truly important in my life, and what was just tiddlywinks. Today that word is more often used as a descriptor meaning trivial or unimportant…small potatoes.

During the nights, Bill would call me over to tend to a physical need with a gentle request and a thank you when done. My favorite was when he called to turn him from one side to the other. This involved propping his back with a pillow for comfort. It included a nice long, gentle backrub. The love that filled the room in those moments left me in awe. We laughed a lot during this time. We joked about human biological malfunctions, often his. We joked lovingly about old guys and cars and crazy people.

Sitting in a big recliner next to Bill each night, I thought about the events, accomplishments, defeats of my own life. I tip-in for the game-winning basket against the cross town rivals. A wink in the pot. I catch double pneumonia a week before the state playoffs. A bad wink. The school I run is named the top of its kind in the state. A wink in the pot. I am removed from my job. A bad wink. I win a speech contest. A wink in the pot. My latest novel gets another rejection slip. A bad wink.

I realized that so much of what I thought was important in my life was, in fact, just tiddlywinks.

Yet, what I remember about the real game was the laughter, the cheers when anyone's wink landed in the pot. We would smile at each other and cheer for the guy with the squidger. In those moments when our love transcends the game itself, that's the good stuff, the real deal, the smiles. Not the straining effort to prove ourselves right or better or worthy. That's tiddlywinks. Smiles require no proof.

Each night, Bill asked me to read a passage from Robert Holden's book, *Holy Shifts*. Bill studied the Course in Miracles upon which the book was based. On his final night, Bill had me read a passage from that book. After a long pause, he asked me to read it a second time and became very quiet. Shortly after midnight, Bill asked me to turn him and I gave him a nice, long backrub. As always, Bill ended the session with, "Thank you, Pat." Then Bill became quiet.

And if I should die before I wake, I pray the Lord my soul to take.

Five minutes later, I could no longer hear Bill breathing. I checked carefully, and when I was certain he had passed, I simply said, "God Bless you Bill." That's when I felt grateful for my dad's childhood prayer. I knew Bill's soul was in good hands.

His soul to keep.

From Bill, I learned that since we all play some kind of tiddlywinks in life, let's play it like we used to when we were kids. Let's play for the smiles, for the love we share with each other, for that spiritual connection which lasts far beyond all life's tiddlywinks.

29

HEROES

Hard times do not create heroes.
It is in hard times that the hero within us
is revealed.

-Bob Riley

When the largest fire in California history tore through our area in the winter of 2017, heroes emerged. A couple of months later, road signs of thanks still dot the sides of Highway 33 and throughout the Ojai Valley thanking the thousands of firemen, policemen and others who literally saved this valley from a raging fire that completely encircled it. One of those firemen lost his life to that fire.

These days, I still can't sit in a coffee shop in

Ojai for very long without hearing another story from an Ojai resident, who, in their own way, became another hero of the fire. Something about flames stopping at our doorstep not only humbles us, but also fills us with gratitude, and reminds of that which is truly important in our lives.

One such hero has worn the wedding ring I put on her finger for over forty-five years. My wife Margaret's story actually begins days before the fire. She drove me to my knee replacement surgery and sat by my side through a rough beginning to my recovery. The day after my surgery, when I tried to stand for physical therapy, I collapsed. Later that day, a second attempt ended quickly with me in extreme pain, blood pressure dropping and an intense panic attack. I just knew that I was dying. Margaret held my hand with a steady, solid love.

Quite some time later, I calmed a bit. Margaret kept her steady eyes on my face and saw something. "What are you feeling right now?" she asked.

I blurted out, "I don't want to die all alone like my dad!" And I broke into deep, healing sobs.

When peace settled inside, I turned to her, still shaking a bit, and asked if she would please stay with me at the hospital that night. She slept on a couch-bed beside me. The next day I was able to do the physical therapy and go home.

I can't remember ever feeling so dependent upon another human being in my life. I was used to being the strong one. This totally vulnerable role was hard to give in to, but I had no choice. When I tried to step out of that role, "Sergeant Pain" would instantly correct my behavior. For days, Margaret, in addition to doing all of the chores, cooked for me, brought me ice packs, medicine, fluids. She helped my lift my leg onto the bed. She cared for me 24/7. The pain gradually receded in the healing of her loving care.

One morning, after a power outage in the night, just after she'd served me breakfast in my recliner in the living room, a knock at the door jarred us. A neighbor stood in our doorway with a stern look.

"There's a fire. It's bad. We all need to evacuate." Behind him, the entire sky glowed like a bright orange wall. A few more words were exchanged ending with him saying, "I'll check back with you to make sure you leave before we leave."

I overheard the conversation and instantaneously, my knee pain shot up to off the charts. Not only was I helpless, I felt useless.

Hearing my moans, Margaret rushed back to give me a dose of the heavy duty pain meds. She sat quietly for a moment in the chair across from me, prayed, and listened. The message came quickly and clearly. *Leave now.* While tending to my pain and other needs, my wife, single-handedly packed two suitcases, important documents, the laptops, the rehab gear for me, various other treasured and needed items and two pet crates for Nina, our black dog, and Emma, our gray tabby cat.

She lost it briefly when the cat ran under the bed and refused to come out. She yelled to the cat, "I'm trying to save your life! If you don't come out of there you're going to die in a fire! Please, kitty. Please, Please. Please." In very un-cat-like behavior, the cat came right out and walked into her arms.

Turning off the gas and electricity, I hobbled into our completely-filled van, spoke a prayer and said goodbye to our home. Margaret drove down our driveway to bumper-to-bumper traffic on the road that led to the only clear highway exit. For forty miles, we crept on that highway behind an endless line of cars with clouds of reddened smoke billowing not far off. Because the narrow, hilly road wound back and forth, it often looked like we were driving right into the flames.

Our radio didn't work in those hills, so, we could only rely on occasional text messages as to our status. Our kids in L.A. and England texted us constantly. Two hours later we emerged on the coastal highway that would take us to our daughter's home in L.A. The heavy weight of doubt lifted. Surely the 101 would safely take us to L.A. Ironically, in the aftermath of the fire, days later, even that coastal highway was closed due to treacherous, killer mudslides.

The trip down the coast took us another five challenging hours. I couldn't get under the pain and the stress to sleep, so I handled navigation and updates on the smart phone. Margaret had to be exhausted, but all I could see on her face was the loving determination of a mother lion, committed to prevail through all of this.

I still do not like being so dependent upon anyone. But if I have to be, I would choose no one else to care for me. As I did forty-five years ago, I would choose my wife, Margaret Peake, my greatest hero!

30

FINDING HOPE

If I could tell the world just one thing
It would be that we are all okay.

-Jewel

These days it seems quite easy to view someone as the enemy: a political leader, a shooter, a terrorist. For many, I suspect it feels futile. What do we do about them? Are we actually helpless? Do we have to just endure the pain they inflict upon us, upon others? Is it all... *hopeless*?

Hopeless. That word triggers a memory from a time in my life when I thought my world was ending. My beloved wife had contracted meningitis, an often fatal and very painful disease. In the Army, I remembered guys taken from our barracks with it, who never returned. What she experienced was extreme pain. Like someone had stabbed a red hot poker down her spine. There seemed to be nothing we could do. We saw countless doctors and healers, and nothing worked.

She endured this for over a year. For over a year I wondered if I would ever have my wife back. For over a year she wondered if she would ever have her life back. Our enemy seemed unrelenting and beyond our ability to do anything about it. It awoke us in the middle of the night, greeted us every morning, and spent the day with us. I was literally brought to my knees. Besides listening to her and holding her, I felt lost. I asked, "Lord, what more can I do?"

I heard a three-part answer.

The first was to continue to spend time on my knees, praying.

Second, every day, when she found the relief of sleep, I was to sit quietly with the intention of deeply listening inside. In there, I heard a clear message: *Take heart, take heart, my beloved. All is well.* Crazy as it sounds, during that hour of meditation each day, I knew that all *was* well. I knew my beloved was in good hands, and I knew that no matter what the outcome, we were blessed.

Third, I gave my wife long foot rubs. My wife and I received a book called *Foot Reflexology* for a wedding gift. It was the best gift ever. Many days I rubbed her feet for about an hour and eased her pain. In those moments, I felt my wife's powerful loving essence behind the mask of meningitis. It was the same loving essence I felt as she cared for me after my spinal surgery. My world did not end.

You may think that it's easy for me to say all this. She lived. She healed. But the truth is I knew she was in good hands either way. I have buried my first son from my first marriage who died hours after birth. I have watched my first grandson die in his father's arms. I have experienced a student shooting and killing another student at my school. And my world did not end.

In the world out there, the upset, the sense of hopelessness, the enemies of good sense seem to abound.

Without excusing, nor making small the devastation they may have caused, I'd like to suggest that all of them actually may have forgotten who they truly are, because of their own deep, secret pain.

Henry Wadsworth Longfellow said, "If we could read the secret history of our enemies, we should find in each man's life sorrow and suffering enough to disarm all hostility."

That political leader, that shooter, that terrorist. I doubt if they would be interested in my offer of a foot rub. But I can honor the essence of their humanity sometimes hidden deeply inside, hidden even from themselves. I can be civil and respectful, even as I clearly oppose and take action against their cause, not with malice, but with charity and strength of heart. I can listen in silence for the higher perspective, the compassion, even for those who have demonstrated so little of it for others, for those who've replaced compassion with revenge.

Here's the thing. Are my *own* actions to be guided by compassion or by revenge? Do I want to heal the wounds of the world with the tools of retribution, or the tools of the heart? As hard as this may be to see, amidst all the horrific words and actions in the world, all the seemingly senseless loss, I find myself continuing to strive for that higher perspective, that place where I remember the loving essence in each of us, and in that Light, know that...

All is well.

31

BEST FRIEND

A friend is one that knows you as you are
Understands where you have been,
Accepts what you have become, and still,
Gently allows you to grow.

-William Shakespeare

It started with a dream. My best friend is trapped in a cave. He's being held in there by some strange mechanical device. The cave is in a cliff by the ocean and cannot be reached because of the crashing waves. Yet, I receive a hand-written note from him, "Please come."

The morning after my dream, I called my best friend, Robert Moreno. I told him the dream. On the day before my dream, they took him to the dentist, held his jaws open with some strange mechanical device and poured water in his mouth. To Robert, a man who'd nearly drowned, a man who is now quadriplegic from a body surfing accident, a man who was not supposed to live, that ordeal with the dentist was terrifying. He didn't sleep much that night.

"Can I come?"

I had to ask. The last time I called to invite myself, his wife, Chachi, said no because he was in too much pain.

This time, though still in that pain, he wanted to see me. A few days later, I drove 250 miles back to Calexico.

One of Robert's new forms of entertainment was watching what he referred to as "TV comedy," otherwise known as the national news. He watches from his very cool, totally adjustable, electronic wheelchair. Chachi tells me he sits all day in a special, semi-supine position, his knees and torso raised, creating the least amount of pain.

We spent the whole afternoon talking. His

broad face grinned as we shared our stories. He sat there decked out in his Pendleton shirt, buttoned to the top button like the *vatos* on the street. The shirttails draped on the outside of carefully-pressed khaki slacks. He didn't look much like an ex-superintendent of schools.

It being March Madness, the NCAA basketball finals, we remembered our exploits on a basketball team together. We played on an educator's team *not* known for their ability to be good sport role models. Some of our teammates played for blood. Literally like get-them-on-the-ground-and-punch-them-in-the-face blood. Robert and I were the good guys on our team. In elementary school, we'd be the ones the teacher puts the unruly kid in the desk beside in hopes we'd be a calming influence.

With all that behind us, we talked about life now. Two older men, he mostly paralyzed from the neck down, working hard to develop some mobility, and me, full of bionic parts replacements. What was our purpose now? I told him what I noticed was the continual flow of family and friends into their abode to visit

Robert, to simply be in his home. I conjectured that maybe he is here, now, as a lighthouse for their loving. It beckons friends and relatives to visit, to have an opportunity to transcend their own troubles in loving service. Maybe that's Robert's destiny, and maybe it's mine as well now.

The best parts of my visit were two foot rubs. I'd told Robert that I was able to relieve some of my wife's pain when she struggled with meningitis by rubbing her feet. He asked me to try it with him.

"Do you have feeling in your feet, Robert?"

He wiggled his toes.

His caretaker set him up on his bed. I pulled up a chair. After squirting lotion on my hands, I rubbed them together and took hold of a foot. Right away I could feel the spots on the sole that corresponded to the pain centers in his body. My study and practice of foot reflexology served me well. Softly at first and then more firmly, I smoothed the bundled muscles in each foot and within an hour he told me he had no pain. None. Actually, I knew I had little to do with what happened here. I felt larger hands guiding mine.

I went to my motel that night to rest and the next morning I was up early for a Denny's Senior Special and a fishing trip. I caught two huge catfish in the canals of the Imperial Valley, and, in keeping with the tradition started years ago, I brought the fillets to Robert and Chachi that morning.

Robert told me he experienced the best sleep he'd had in months and was hoping to get another foot rub before I left. I was alone with Robert for one more foot rub. Words cannot describe the Light that was in that room as I worked on his feet.

Halfway through, I heard Robert snoring. I hoped his dreams were uplifting this time. My heart filled with gratitude for my friend. Standing at the foot of the bed of this sleeping angel, whispering a prayer, I gently held both feet in my hands. Words came to me from a spiritual reading. As I released his feet, his eyes opened and he simply said.

"I love you, Pat."

I feel so blessed to have received the note

Robert passed to me in my dream, and so grateful I had, like the good student, followed directions.

Robert, thanks for the reminder. Like it says in the book, "Love endures all things."

32

YOUR SONG

The calm mind allows one to connect with the
inner self, the Soul, the very source of being.
That's where the music lives...

-Clarence Clemons

What is your song? I'm not talking about your favorite hit. I'm talking about your song, the one inside you. That one.

In 1981, I began a search for this song in a service project for a college psychology class at the University of Santa Monica. I chose a convalescent hospital. Maybe I could learn from my elders. What a concept.

I remember the first day I attended. Beside the distinct smell, I remember the lost look on a lady's face as she looked up at me from her wheelchair and said, "Can you help me?"

Well, I thought, *I was born to help others.*

"Can you push me to my room?"

I took hold of those wheelchair handles with the conviction of Mother Theresa, and began pushing. She looked up at me, urgency in her eyes. "Faster."

I thought, *Oh no, bathroom!* I kicked it into high gear.

Whooshing down the hall, her long, grey hair blown back, she raised her arms above her head and hollered, "Wheeeeee!"

I had been played.

Despite my ignominious beginning, I continued serving. I even brought my young son and daughter on the weekends for backup.

From then until now, I continued my search with the elderly, especially with those who seemed to have checked out. I listen for their song, too.

I'll bet you all already know exactly what I am talking about because you too have experienced someone's song. You've heard their song even when they are grumbling about the "whatevers" of life.

Nowadays, I log in at a local care center. I must admit that I am there for me. I receive so much more than I give. However, my partner, my dog Nina, is there for everybody. One of our friends, Trudy, had advanced MS and couldn't position her distorted body to see Nina from her permanent and painful stay in bed. Nina would hop up and put two paws on her bed so Trudy could stroke her soft ears. Though Trudy recently passed on, I still hear her beautiful song as I picture her stroking Nina's ears.

Another patient, Pearl, wheeled her chair out to the smoking patio cussing up a blue streak and sobbing, screaming for her momma. I sat with my friends Marlene and Pedro who assured me that Pearl's momma died a few months ago and that her MS condition had turned her grief into rage. Marlene, full of her own health challenges, hollered at Pearl. "Shut up!"

Of course this was met by an even more furious barrage of obscenities accompanied by obscene gestures. I shared with my two friends how my daughter Lisa, at six years old, once stopped a screamer like that in her tracks. "How?" Pedro asked.

"Let me see if I can show you. Nina, stay."

I waltzed over to Pearl. I admit I was a little nervous as I pulled up a chair.

"Hi, Pearl."

"Hi, Pat."

I simply sat very still, meeting her eyes, listening. She grew calm as she studied my face and she spoke some kind words. It wasn't her words that touched me so deeply. It was her sweet song – inside her.

The way Pearl's song came to me was as if I sat alone in the front row of Carnegie Hall. From the orchestra pit, a single violin sweetly greeted me. A spotlight appeared center stage, illuminating her silver hair, and an alto voice filled the hall with a glorious aria that sent chills all over my body and lifted my heart to tears of joy.

All this, from inside Pearl.

When I started these visits, I was thirty-five. I am now seventy-five. Old. I think about what might happen if I come to a point where I've checked out. Will I be sad? Angry? Afraid? Maybe. But I have learned something from my friends at the care center. This is what I know:

There is a beautiful song inside each of us. We've sung our song together with loved ones many times. Our song continues no matter what. If you take the time to become still and listen carefully, you can hear my song and I can hear yours.

If I become like my friends at the care center, when you visit me, you may have some difficulty hearing me because of all that has happened to my personality, my body, my mind. Perhaps the luster will go out of my eyes. Perhaps I'll be sad, angry, afraid. Perhaps I'll no longer know who you are. It can be very distracting. No worries. I will still be in here. Stroke my head, hold my hand, listen...not for what I may or may not say. Listen for the song. If you live far away, you can still carry me in your heart, you can still hear my song. You can be on the other side of the world, and, if you think of me, listen carefully. You may even hear a message.

I invite you to take a moment right now, to

picture the loving face of a special elder in your life, living or not. Like the song that inspired this writing, this could be your song to them, or their song to you:

I hope you don't mind. I hope you don't mind
that I put down in words. How wonderful life is
that you're in the world.

Just listen.

33

WHO ARE WE?

God enters by a private door into
every individual.

-Ralph Waldo Emerson

As a young boy, I looked into the eye of the Great Blue Heron and found God. Sitting on a creek bank beside this bird, I became aware of the immensity of life. Since then, I have been on a quest to answer a simple question.

"Who am I? "

That translates into, "Who are we?"

As a college student, I began to find an answer to that question, not in the classroom, but while sitting at a typewriter, a little after midnight at the summer camp for special needs kids. I had an experience—the first of several similar experiences—which remind me of our true nature.

Because it was the kids' first experience away from home for a whole week, I was on duty round the clock. At three in the morning, a tug at my arm by a small hand reminded me of this. Camper Stevie told me he heard a voice out in the woods. It kept asking him *who, who, who?*

In addition to my commitment to the boys, I was given an additional job. The camp director found out I was editor of my college newspaper and "volunteered" me to create a camp newsletter to give to the parents at week's end. That meant late night interviews with the other counselors and typing, editing, copying. Our teen assistants would look after the sleeping campers.

The young men and women counselors I interviewed were so dedicated, so loving. It was an honor to work with them. That last night, I was putting the finishing touches on the newspaper around midnight. I had just written a poem for the paper about the gift these children bring us, about the pure light of love in their eyes. Several counselors were there with me. We laughed about the funny moments we had with our kids. I shared my epic worm race story. I can still see their gleaming eyes as every one of my campers watched with great anticipation for the entire half hour it took for the winning worm to make the ten inch trek to the edge of the circle. You'd think the winner had won gold at the Olympics. All the others were patting the winning worm's owner on the back and cheering.

That night at the workroom, our sides were aching with that kind of hysterical laughter that happens when you've worked too hard and stayed up too late. I was at my typewriter, barely able to read the type because of the tears of laughter in my eyes. Flashes of sweet moments with the kids filled my heart. My own life issues seemed so trivial as I witnessed the great love in my boys' eyes.

Then it happened. I became pure laughter, pure joy. My physical body, as I knew it, disappeared. I felt literally like I had no body. And yet, I was filled with so much joy. The only thing I could see was a beautiful white light surrounding me. It no longer mattered where I was or what I was doing or who I thought I was.

I had to rely on the reports of my fellow counselors about what happened to my missing body while I was experiencing this out-of-body joy. They told me that I finished the newspaper, got up, and walked off into the middle of the woods, not even a trail. Two of them ran after me and tried to talk to me but all I could do was grin at them. They guided my body to my cabin and laid me down on my cot.

As I was lying on my back on my cot, I heard a voice coming out of my thick white cloud. "Are you going to be okay?"

"Sure," I said. "I'm just fine."

I had even had the presence of mind to check that my campers and teen assistant were sound asleep. But then, I closed my eyes.

A slide show of images raced across my inner vision at a rate of ten pictures per second. I could barely make them out, but occasionally I saw something: Face after face flashed, of friends, family, teachers, heroes in my life. Special faces, spiritual teachers, some long passed, like Jesus,

Buddha, others I hadn't yet met. The show ended with blasts of light in gold, green, purple and white.

As tears of gratitude dripped down my face, I thought, *Well, I am pretty sure I am having a psychotic break of some sort. I might as well go to sleep since tomorrow I am probably going to wake up in a mental hospital. But this sure feels amazing.*

It wasn't until years later that I began to truly understand the gift that had been given to me that night. I have experienced enough similar transcendent moments since then to know that this was quite real. In my studies with my spiritual teacher, John Roger, and in my classes and service in the spiritual psychology program at the University of Santa Monica, I have found a deepening inner awareness of the truth of who I am.

Recently, I had a profound reunion with my True Self during an extremely high risk surgery on my spine. When I returned to this world from that place, nurses, doctors, and family were all surprised at my joy and acceptance of this new journey in my life. As with the Blue Heron and the camp counseling experience, I found myself in a deep and loving connection with what is sometimes referred to as the "greater within me." In there, all is not only well, it is also a blessing, a gift beyond anything of this world.

As with that Great Blue Heron, I had been given a door to walk through to see who was *really* the guy behind the curtain. The key to the door was, and always is, pure love.

At that camp, that night, I felt such a profound love. I was given a glimpse of who I really am, who we all are. Words fall short of the experience itself, way short. Behind the door of personality, we are all divine beings, we are all souls, we are all the Light, we are all that pure love.

If they were here, I'll bet my Down syndrome boys would just be laughing at me right now. They already know this. In their own way, I think maybe they've always known who we really are.

The thing is, I forget. We all forget. But we are reminded over and over of this truth, in the stories of heroes, in the face of nurses, in the hands of healers, in the embraces of friends and family, in the words of poets, in the eyes of babies, always there, between the headlines, reminding us of the real truth of who we are.

34

THE ANSWER WITHIN

*At the center of your being you have the answer;
you know who you are and you know what
you want.*

-Lao Tzu

Why is this happening to me?

There are a group of questions that I call, "key questions." They are questions whose answers may unlock doors of self-discovery, questions for which there seem to be no easy answer, questions like, *Now what do I do? Why am I here? Where am I going?*

Books have been written to answer these questions. Motivational speakers have devoted their lives to sharing their answers. And almost everyone has an opinion and advice to give you about them.

I'd like to offer you a story of my own search for answers to such questions. Actually, it began long ago as a child, in moments of solitude. Things around my home sometimes became quite noisy with the clamor of three active children, a mom who drank too much, a dad who worked too much, a grandma, and aunts and uncles all living in a three-story white house on a corner of a small Iowa town. Most of the noise was joyful, but a good portion of it was challenging, especially on those nights when the adults would fight.

I would wake up around two in the morning after everyone was asleep, sneak out of bed, sit in the big recliner in the living room, and read, write, and draw. I read classic excerpts from a book called *Gems for the Fireside*. Wordsworth, Poe, Frost, and many others. I would write poems that strained to rhyme. I would open encyclopedias and sketch old sailing ships and airplanes. As I did, I would become quite still inside. As a teen, I would spend countless hours away from home, staring at my fishing pole or my line slicing into the water or a Great Blue Heron fishing in the reeds. In that stillness, I began to find answers.

Over the years, through my studies, workshops, amazing classes in spiritual psychology and my own spiritual practices, I have found a place inside myself where I can always count on finding the answers to the key questions.

Recently, one of those big questions burned in my spine and knocked my legs out from under me. The question was: *Why is this happening to me?*

At the time I was in a weekend class at the University of Santa Monica. Over and over during the weekend, when I would inwardly ask this question, I consistently got back the same answer: This is a test.

What test?

By the end of that weekend, my legs were wobbly. I draped my arms around the shoulders of two strong assistants to get from the classroom to the car. Two days later I was lying on a hospital gurney at the University of Southern California's Keck Hospital awaiting emergency spinal surgery. A cancerous tumor had formed on my T7 vertebra causing a compression fracture. We were told that this was a high risk surgery but that my surgeon only performed high risk surgeries.

I asked the anesthesiologist to please give me ten minutes before he gave me the drug that would put me under. Everyone there was so kind and accommodating. I closed my eyes and listened within and watched. In a profound, sacred and very private experience, I got my answer to the question about the test.

The answer came very clearly. But first I heard the results of my test. I passed. The test was for me, with my whole being, to embrace total acceptance of *either* result of my surgery.

Before that moment, I had worries about my family. I hadn't been willing to let them go. On that gurney, I became very clear about two things:

If I passed on, my family and friends would be sad, but they would be fine and even blessed with greater loving in their lives. And I would be blessed beyond words.

If I stayed, I would have the opportunity to share my love even more fully with them and many others. And I would be blessed beyond words.

I was wheeled into my surgery feeling a deep joy and gratitude for either result.

Approximately nine hours later, through blurry eyes, I saw a long intubation tube being slowly extracted from my throat. A young angel of a nurse was at my side. "Welcome back, Mr. Peake. Breathe."

As the tube parted from my throat I took a deep, gentle breath which felt like the first breath of my life. It was the sweetest air I'd ever tasted.

So here I am…back.

After four weeks in the hospital, we drove into the green hills of the Ojai Valley, and I had never seen anything more beautiful in my life. I came back with so much more than I had left with. So much more.

Every day, I return to that place within for not only answers to the key questions, but simple guidance as to what to put on my plate for the day. I feel honored to be here, knowing that besides having so much to give, I have so much to learn. I am, after all, still a human being, living on this planet, ready to take the next test, and experience the next blessing.

35

CALLING ALL ANGELS

You were born with wings, why prefer to crawl through life?

-Rumi

Almost two years ago, I began seeing angels. Real angels. Some didn't even know they were angels. But I did — because I was their client

On the night of February 14, 2018, after being rushed to USC Keck Hospital, I had cancerous tumors removed from my spine and my vertebrae rebuilt with a spinal fusion.

In a profound inner experience, just before the surgery, I discovered a new way of seeing. I could spot them. And they were everywhere.

After nine hours of surgery, I met my first angel

early the next morning. As a long intubation tube was withdrawn from my throat she said, "Welcome back, Mr. Peake. Breathe."

It was the sweetest breath I had ever taken. It felt like it was the first breath of my life. In a way, it was. The angel welcoming me into my new life, Asha, looked so young. But her eyes sparkled with the wisdom of the ages.

In contrast, two floors below, in the recovery section, Barb, carried a frown on her face. Yet she efficiently did her job with a minimum of personal contact. Her face seemed fixed in stone.

One day, Barb came in by herself, sticking her cellphone in her pocket and her stone face cracking. I knew she was one, I just knew it.

We made eye contact, and I asked her how she was doing. The tears came with the story of a domestic struggle that had her feeling tied up in knots. The knots unraveled as she told her story, and I could see the brilliant Light of the angel she had been hiding. And so could she.

One more floor down, I am pretty sure my physical therapists, Ray and Jen, had no idea of their divine gift. Oh, I think they knew they were good physical therapists but weren't aware of the bright light that they carried with them. As they pushed me to step up my game, we would chat to keep up my spirits. Jen and I talked about basketball. Ray and I talked about fishing.

They both were surprised to have me show up three months later, walking with a cane. "I just came for the hugs," I announced, and I got to remind them of their gift.

I could go on... Kathy, my physical therapist in Ojai, Theresa, my chemo nurse, Rene, my support group leader at Ojai Cares, all the massage therapists there, and my favorite angel of all and best friend, my wife, Margaret. And here's the funny part. They know that I know who they really are and still sometimes forget, or pretend not to know.

So here is my prayer. I am, right now, calling all angels to awaken inside yourselves and remember your true identity. Not only you, health care provider, you teacher, writer, you cashier, mechanic, lawyer, mom, dad. You grandparent, you best friend. You know who you are.

If you still think you don't, let me remind you of the time you held a person's hand who was in distress. Let me remind you of a child whose face lit up when they saw you. Let me remind you of the kind words you spoke when someone needed to hear them. Let me remind you of the hard times when you gave up some personal comfort to comfort another.

I am calling all angels to awaken, for when we do, we light up and heal the troubled places of our world, the dark places, even the ones inside ourselves.

Arise angels. We need you.

You really do know who you are.

EPILOGUE

The first seventy-five years of my life seem like a blink in time. From a higher perspective, they truly are. My stories are snapshots in a photo album, like that picture of the Great Blue Heron standing beside me as a boy. They are glimpses into what has stirred my heart.

In every single story I told here, there was always one physical element common to each. In every one of these, I remember some special person's eyes. Often, I found a sacred light in those eyes, just as Mr. Hearst had seen my Light.

I see my beloved Margaret in that moment on a mountain ledge where I fell in love with those twinkling brown eyes. And in that moment of terror, when I almost lost her to the sea. And each breakfast when I listen to her tell her plans for the day and what to do about that special child who complicates her classroom.

I see Robert's eyes in the first moments of

his birth and how I found God in them.

I feel the arm of Lisa linked in mine, sunlight gleaming in her eyes, as we march down the grassy aisle to her loving groom.

I watch Alan, the Down syndrome boy, looking up at me with a big grin on his face when I discovered that, contrary to what he led me to believe, he could tie his own shoe. He just didn't want to until that moment.

I spot Lydia in my first classroom, gazing at me with serious green eyes as I began to understand the huge responsibility of being a teacher.

I watch Alfonso rubbing the design on the dresser he made for his grandma and making himself visible to the world during a time of great loss.

I see Bud's eyes, filled with the orange sunset on his last earthly fishing trip.

I watch Mr. Hearst, gazing into a field of corn and talking with me about the meaning of life.

I hear Pearl's beautiful song inside as she gazes at me with vulnerable eyes at the care center.

I feel my quadriplegic friend, Robert, watching me with loving eyes as I give him a foot rub.

I hear Bill's faint voice thanking me as he closes his eyes after his last earthly back rub.

I see the purple and gold of a Minnesota lake at sunset reflected in my dad's eyes as he shows us God in the beauty of Nature.

I hear Mom singing that Irish lullaby to me as an earthbound angel and another beautiful song as a heavenly angel.

I see my grandson, Luca, smiling with eyes full of light and joy, eating blueberries beside me at the breakfast table.

I feel the hands of Jesus on my shoulders, rubbing my back where the surgery was, reminding me, by example, of our true purpose, to love all and to be of service.

As Juan taught me, in the end, only kindness matters. It's all about loving.

Blessings of Loving and Light to you.

ACKNOWLEDGEMENTS

It's my sincere wish that this book in itself will be an acknowledgement to all the people who have been part of this journey, the people I speak about as I tell these stories. Of course, some of the names have been changed intentionally in respect for their privacy. In addition, there have been so many who have been there in support of this work who are equally as important to me.

I must first mention my writer's group, The Ojai Scribes, with whom I have met weekly for over fifteen years. In particular, I'd like to thank the longest-standing members and three ladies who've been with me almost all of that time: Anne Boydston, LaNette Donoghue, and Pat Hartmann. And I'd like to thank our newest member, Dena Hayess Horton.

I must also thank all my Ojai Toastmasters who have cheered me on as I have given every one of these stories as a speech, often in the International Inspirational Speech Contests over the past twelve years. And, of course, my wife, Margaret, who has not only helped me with the first edits of these, but has endured hearing them rehearsed over and over in our home.

I want to thank my awesome editor Jim Martyka, who not only provided excellent technical support on the writing itself, but the moral support for the value of this work.

In acknowledgement of the people who have been important in my self-discovery process, I must begin with Drs. Ron and Mary Hulnick, the president and vice president of the University of Santa Monica. They've held me in their hearts for over thirty-five years, as I have them. I have been with them as student, assistant, facilitator, reader, and faculty member throughout this time.

And finally, I want to thank my spiritual teachers Jesus Christ, John-Roger, and John Morton for always being there for me, no matter what my external circumstances were, and reminding me to keep stepping up to the higher ground. Thank you.

ABOUT PAT

Pat has touched the lives of students from kindergarten to graduate-level college. His wife, son, and daughter have been inspired by hundreds of stories he would tell them. It all started at age eight when he would tell nightly stories to his younger brother and sister when they all slept in the same room.

Now, he writes them.

ADDITIONAL BOOKS BY PATRIC PEAKE

CHAIN MAIL MAN

Excerpts from the novel's Advance Praise section include:

"Every boy longs for a father's love. And even the toughest emotional chain mail can't hide a recluse from the earnest heart of the searcher. Neither the emotional toll of war nor the protective instincts of a mother can keep Henry McQuiddy from learning the truth about his missing dad and discovering the bonds they still share."

" ... an exhilarating journey of discovery and adventure ..."

"... a heart-rending look at a journey of the soul and the bittersweet rewards of not giving up ... no matter what."

Chain Mail Man is available in paperback and ebook.

Two of Pat's books are available on his website. You're invited to take a digital stroll and enjoy them.

http://patricpeake.com

MAGIC PENCIL GIRL

Listen to an audiobook of a sixth-grade girl who has lost her dad and is negotiating through a rocky time in elementary school with the assistance of her magic pencil. When she draws something with it, and taps the drawing, it comes alive!

INSPECTOR PEPPER

Read murder mysteries that were designed originally for people with memory loss. Hence the subtitle: "From Crime to Cuffs in less than 10 minutes. This tongue-in-cheek crime series is just a fun read.